Go Big or Go Home

The

NEWSMAKER

A Leadership Story of
Honor and Love

John

Be the change!

Tony Bridwell

Author of *The Maker* Series

"Once again, Tony Bridwell has created a moving story about living on purpose with integrity and love for others. Proof that we can lead lives with courage and kindness that will change lives and make a positive impact in our community."

Lynne Stewart
Owner/President, SUPERIORHIRE

"Tony produced another page-turner book! Rooted in love, forgiveness, and honor, this read will inspire you to continue your journey of purpose."

Tiffany Haynes
General Manager of HR, Jack Henry & Associates

"With *The Newsmaker*, Bridwell tells a most captivating story while challenging the reader with the question, 'what would be different in your life story if you lead with love?' An inspiring read of courage and faith."

Jean Leger
VP of Utility Operations, OG&E

"Tony Bridwell once again delivers thought-provoking insights through powerful and engaging storytelling in *The Newsmaker*. We find ourselves deeply connected to the characters, who are faced with life's toughest challenges and heart-wrenching choices. By skillfully weaving in characters and lessons from *The Kingmaker*, we are reminded that these struggles provide meaning to our personal journey, but, more importantly, can make the difference in the lives of others. By leading with love, honor, and forgiveness, we are all empowered to #BeTheChange."

Talia Salvati
Founder & Chief Talent Officer, uplift HR

"Brilliant! *The Newsmaker* is a suspenseful and heartfelt story that masterfully illustrates the importance of purpose and leadership in your life. The story will have you sitting on the edge of your seat, and reflecting on how you can positively impact others and make a difference in the world."

Amy L. Ross
CEO & Founder, HumanKind HR

"In today's fast-paced environment, we don't often take time to reflect on our purpose in life and how we choose to show up as leaders. Bridwell pulls us into the story of Carson Stewart, who deals with some major life lessons while figuring out what it means to live with purpose, integrity, and service. You can't help but reflect on your own journey and what changes you may want to consider that will make you a better leader and person."

Kate Terrell
CHRO, Driscoll's

"*The Newsmaker* is a powerful book with an exciting storyline. Within the pages are the threads of beautiful examples of love and forgiveness. Tony really encourages the reader to do a bit of soul-searching within themselves. Wonderful book!"

Tara Storch
Co-Founder, Taylor's Gift Foundation

"The human condition requires a delicate balance and *The Newsmaker* takes the reader of this beautifully told modern fable on a full-circle view of the impactful and positive change that comes from giving, receiving, and making the most of second chances. Read this book—and see what happens when we choose to truly lead with love and forego judgment of others based on circumstances or external appearances. Tony Bridwell IS The Newsmaker!"

Brad K. Wardlow
VP of People and Culture, Makeready

"Tony Bridwell continues to amaze me with his latest install-ment in *The Maker* series. In *The Newsmaker*, he perfectly de-picts a story of someone who has fallen from a position of influence and power but is beautifully restored through a path of humility and integrity. A great reminder for any leader."

John Luke Spitler
President/CEO, The Encompass Group

"*The Newsmaker* provides a striking picture of the hazards of leading with a focus on 'self-first.' This book teaches an important lesson that real influence is not about job titles or headlines, but develops from leading with moral courage, humility, and a purposeful commitment to serve those around us."

Laura Schilling
President, Pumpco Services Inc

"This story reveals extraordinary leadership principles. It demonstrates the powerful impact that choosing to lead with love, forgiveness, and serving others in ways that dignify and honor them can bring. This book, and Tony, inspires and challenges me to be a better leader."

Amanda Hite
Co-Founder and CEO, Be The Change Revolutions

"It is too easy to default to prescribed definitions of success, whether dictated by societal norms or one's own expectations. With *The Newsmaker*, Tony Bridwell reminds us how finding our purpose can re-center our journey, replacing void achievement with fulfillment and meaning."

Steve Smith
Partner and Chief Operating Officer, Firehouse

"This book is a crazy ride. It had unexpected twists and turns in the story line and I was completely blown away at how Tony seamlessly connected *The Newsmaker* with his previous book, *The Kingmaker*. Not only does Tony masterfully tell a story, but he weaves inspiring life and leadership principles throughout the chapters that bring meaning, purpose, and practical application to the reader. As the characters in *The Newsmaker* were learning life lessons, I was making notes in the book margins of things to think through and apply to my own life. This is definitely a book you will be drawn to read, and one I will read again!"

Daniel Morris
Worship Pastor,
Author of *From Survival to Success*

"Bridwell does it again. In *The Newsmaker*, he takes the basic human needs of love and forgiveness, and shows us all the difference you can make if you lead from the heart. The power of purpose in business and in life shines through!"

Kelli Valade
EVP, President, Chili's Grill & Bar

"Tony Bridwell's book is essential if you want to improve your life, and the lives of the people around you—*The Newsmaker: A Leadership Story of Honor and Love* is a must-read!"

Hattie Hill
President and CEO, Women's Foodservice Forum

The

NEWSMAKER

A Leadership Story of
Honor and Love

Tony Bridwell

Author of *The Maker* Series

BᴮB

Copyright © 2017 by Tony Bridwell
Editorial Work: Mindi Bach
Interior Design: Aaron Snethen
Cover Design: Alli Koch (Alli K Design)
Cover Layout: Stephanie Kemp (Sleigh Creative)
Cover Photography Credit:

Typewriter: Tony Bridwell

ISBN: 9780692984734
Library of Congress Control Number: 2017933785

This book is dedicated to my children;
Tyler, Allison, and Brendan, who have been gracious
with me as I continue to learn life.

FOREWORD

As I stepped into a leadership role as chair of an industry orga-
nization, by way of introduction, Tony sent me a signed copy
of his book, *The Kingmaker*, with an inscription in the front
cover that read simply, "Thank you for being a true kingmaker!" Honored and intrigued, I dove into a compelling story
unlike any other I'd read on leadership. Through the personal
journeys of four leaders, Tony brought to life the importance
of leadership, integrity, and purpose, and painted a clear picture that our real outcomes as leaders are not in the results
we deliver but in how we build and guide those around us
to achieve their potential. And that our purpose as leaders is
defined not by title and company, but by the impact we have
on others.

In *The Newsmaker*, the second book of the *Maker* series,
the reader is confronted with leadership choices through a
new industry and lens, this time highlighting the crucible
moments when we have the choice between doing what is
"right"' for us personally or what is simply the right thing to
do. The main character experiences the fallout from a series

of decisions lacking honesty and integrity that disintegrate the things he values most: his reputation, power, influence, and access. As the story unfolds, he reaches a point where the fear of public shame or failure outweighs his guilt. This is the moment when his desire for power becomes personal and not purposeful, and the protagonist spirals to new depths. It is the unconditional love of a mentor, the wise counsel of a friend, and grace from his adversary, that provides the hands to lift him up.

Whether you are a new leader or seasoned executive, a mentor or an apprentice, or a citizen hoping to find integrity in the words of those who lead, *The Newsmaker* is a timely cautionary tale about the pitfalls of success and the desire to maintain an upward trajectory at all costs. Accelerated success and the desire to sustain reputation, can tempt a leader to make desperate, not deliberate, decisions to protect power and position. And in the end, there are times we need other leaders—kingmakers—to remind us of who we are, where we've been, and how we can truly make an impact in the future. Through the "3 Life Choices," this book illustrates the needs in all of us to take inventory of our purpose, our integrity, and the true story written on the pages of our life. It is fitting that this tale also explores unconditional love and the relationships that give leadership the longevity to outlast a career. *The Newsmaker* speaks a newsworthy message to a world weary and wary of rhetoric and status. May this simple fable refresh your desire to listen, to lead, and to follow.

—WENDY DAVIDSON

INTRODUCTION

In an online survey conducted by Goodreads, a site for book readers, it was asked if anyone reads the introduction or preface of a book. To my delight, 90 percent said yes, especially if the introduction is short and interesting. Nothing beats a little pressure to start the day.

The book you are holding is my third book in *The Maker* series. With each book I am asked a simple question; who needs to read this book? As an aspiring author, still a bit naive, the first thought in my head is, of course, everyone. I've learned over the last couple of years that is not always the case.

The Newsmaker is a simple story about a young man struggling in life with the choices he has made and is going to make in the future. His journey, like so many of ours, is complicated. Where *The Kingmaker* brought attention to the importance of having purpose in life, *The Newsmaker* takes the next step to discover how to find your purpose.

Through key characters returning from *The Kingmaker* and new characters introduced in this story, my goal is to provide encouragement to any person who, at times, finds life filled with empty joy. There is a path to a more meaningful life regardless of your situation.

Life has been teaching me a great deal as of late. The core lesson has been around keeping things simple. Gone are my long lists of things to do. In their place I have focused on the few, rarely more than three, things of importance. In *The Newsmaker* you will find three simple ideas, referred to as the 3 Choices. Getting these choices right plays an important part in replacing empty joy with true joy. I'm not naive enough to believe these three choices are the be-all and end-all. No, they are just a starting place.

Our bookstores are filled with volumes of self-help books. Unfortunately, there is no section for "others-help," which is where this book should reside. Our self-first society has been robbing us of the true joy found in an others-first community. It is time for change.

For me, if the world around us needs to change, then I should have the courage to lead the way. Can I confess how scary that sounds? The Good News is I don't have to go alone. My faith teaches me I am never alone. My community of friends ensures that if I stumble, someone will pick me up. What the story of *The Newsmaker* provides is a simple reminder for most that the choices we make do make a difference. So, here we go. The journey begins, and the choices I make today can be the change required for a better tomorrow. It's time to #BeTheChange.

—TONY BRIDWELL

The
STORY

The vibration of the phone had precious little effect on Carson as he hunched over the bar. It did, however, create an elevated Pavlovian response from anyone within earshot. "Hey buddy, you getting that?" mumbled Joe, the slightly irritated bartender, as he set a tall glass of water and a painkiller within Carson's reach.

"Yeah, you going to let that ring all day?" responded the person in the seat closest to Carson. At this point, the throbbing in Carson's head silenced his typical brash response to immediate critics. All Carson wanted was to be left alone so he could self-medicate his current hangover by inducing what was sure to be a monster future hangover.

Hoisting his head from the cradle of his crossed arms, Carson's bloodshot eyes moved between the carefully placed glass of water and a half-empty glass of his favorite whiskey. Today, the choice represented a seemingly accidental metaphor for Carson's life.

The smells of the city were amplified in the small, poorly lit, side-street pub located in Greenwich Village. Anyone entering the establishment was transported back in time. Black and white photographs hung on the wall, many with autographs of the infamous people who had gathered at the bar to share a libation. The soot clinging to a pressed tin ceiling reflected the abundant cigar smoke that filled the room in years past. The bar itself, smooth from decades of cleaning, was a behemoth of carved wood and copper inlay. Its crown jewel, standing as tall and proud as One World Trade in the middle, was the eight-handled beer tap from which local craft beers were poured. Fastened to the mirrored rear wall behind the bar, four shelves of reclaimed wood displayed rows of bottles, reflecting the best spirits the city had to offer. For nearly a century, the bar now known as *Joe's Place*, with its exposed beams and distinctive spirits, has been the quintessential city haven for truth-tellers and secret-keepers; a gathering place for real life characters with stories to tell.

For locals, the preferred seat at *Joe's* was the stool at the end of the bar, which happened to be furthest from the door. The view from this particular seat allowed the occupant an unobstructed view of the entire establishment. For those desiring anonymity, this location allowed for a quick escape down the back stairway, which led to the alley behind the historic building. It was easy to disappear in a place like this, which was precisely what Carson intended. The truth was, millions of readers knew Carson Stewart's story, and that was the one story he was trying to forget.

Given the hour of day, the only person in the bar who knew Carson by name was Joseph Hamilton; "Joe" to the regulars. As owner and bartender of this fine establishment, Joe was once accused of running a dive, to which Joe replied, "I wish this was a dive. This place is just a dump with the hopes of someday becoming a dive."

Joe was a tall, fit man, with close-cropped salt and pepper colored hair accenting his full, thick beard. It seemed the full beard provided him with an inanimate and impenetrable bodyguard. Worn like a mask, his beard allowed him to hide in plain sight, while he navigated the room with his eyes. If eyes could tell a story, his could recount more tales and battles than the journeys of countless men. The piercing blue of the deepest Caribbean waters; his eyes were the lighthouse that led him safely through life's troubled and tranquil seas. His piercing stare exposed a mind shaped by the pages of great literature and the words of poets and philosophers. Shielded by his hardened interior, one glance cut deep into the soul.

He was always dressed in a starched, white shirt buttoned to the top, and dark jeans with a wide leather belt and a simple brass buckle. The slight bulge at his ankle engendered the assumption he was packing heat at all times, but no one ever had the nerve to ask. In addition to his weapon of choice, a Kimber Micro 9mm, Joe was always packing his other preferred weapon, a book. The used bookstore below Joe's Village apartment provided an endless cache of ammunition reloading his thirst for knowledge. A close inspection of the mirrored wall behind the bar revealed an eclectic stack of books, including Nietzsche, Frankl, and Hemingway. His bar library filled his time during the extended periods when patrons were sparse.

Joe's quiet demeanor made him the perfect bartender, but also fueled the mystery of his past. No one really knew his complete story, only bits and pieces compiled over the years. The tattoo, partially exposed when he rolled up his shirtsleeves, provided a clue to his journey. Some suspected the tattoo had a military history, while others claimed it was a dare tattoo from his youth. A simple, well-worn gold ring on his right hand showed signs of faint engraving, possibility from a love lost. The gold band added just one more mystery to Joe's story.

Joe chose his words carefully, but when he did speak, people listened. His ability to tell a story was legendary in the Village. Frequently, you would hear Joe quoting his favorite philosopher or a passage from one of his favorite works, *The Old Man and the Sea*. Hemingway's lessons of courage and strength were abundant in Joe's commentary to his guests.

To only a small, guarded circle, Joe's real superpower was unleashed: his wealth of inside knowledge regarding anybody and anything in the City and beyond. He was a reporter's dream, with resources as vast as the New York City library system. This attracted an elite crowd to gather around his bar in an effort to find the needed angle, quote, or *Deep Throat*-type connection for the next big story. There was never a shortage of writers seated at tables throughout Joe's establishment—each with laptops opened, working to make their story deadline.

During his daily, mid-morning coffee ritual, Joe would scan the press, noting the contributions of key newsmakers from around the country. For Joe, this process wasn't about taking in new information, but more about detecting the misinformation that made it into print. A child of the William Randolph Hearst era of yellow journalism, he was fully attuned to the pressure on good journalists to sacrifice integrity on the altar of ratings and sensationalism. Uncovering a truthful newsmaker was his daily quest, and when he first locked eyes with a young Carson, Joe felt like he had found hope for true integrity in journalism—a hope Joe believed would take Carson to the top of the media world.

Carson first met Joe while in college at NYU. The rumor that *Joe's Place* was a journalistic hangout naturally drew a then-underage Carson to hang with the big boys. The fake ID Carson flashed to Joe on his first visit had been thumbtacked above the "minors will not be served" sign on the wall behind the bar ever since. It was Carson's distinct ability to talk himself out of trouble and charm an audience that impressed Joe during that first encounter. Thankfully, Carson's persuasive abilities only netted him a non-alcohol beer, placed before him until he was of the rightful drinking age. Tragically, alcohol flowed like the East River around campus, allowing Carson other opportunities to fuel his quest to numb the shame he had carried with him for years.

Over time, Carson and Joe's relationship grew beyond just patron and bartender, and Carson considered Joe one of the few people in the world who truly understood him. Carson was never deterred by his multiple visits to *Joe's Place* while underage. In a small, unspoken way, Carson appreciated the one person willing to tell him no.

For the last three months, Carson had been hiding behind the brick walls of Joe's bar. The pressure of the 24-hour news coverage smeared more soot on his reputation than the residue that clung to the tin roof above his head. Carson's troubling condition prompted Joe to carefully guard the clicker for the only flat screen TV in the bar. It remained on the sports channel while Carson was in residence, which lately, was often. Even the customary newspapers and trade pubs were confiscated, replaced with used copies of fictional classics from Hemingway, Fitzgerald, and Twain.

For the fourth time, Carson's phone began to vibrate and bounce across the polished copper bar. Without looking up, Carson felt for his phone. As his fingers curled around the keypad, frustration turned to anger and in a swift motion, he threw the phone across the room. Making contact with the wood and glass framed picture hanging on the wall, the vibration ceased with the resounding crash of glass and metal on the bar floor. For the moment, Carson silenced yet another person hoping to verbally feed on a piece of his flesh, offering temporary solace from the ever-present scrutiny of the press. For Carson, the scrutiny was particularly painful, given that the piranhas nibbling at his phone were formerly part of his fishbowl of colleagues and peers.

Carson's position as a media elite had been well-documented. As a student in NYU's journalism program, Carson quickly defined himself as a prodigy of sorts. His early success opened doors few students had ever achieved. Establishing himself as the youngest nationally syndicated columnist in the country's history, Carson ran with an elite group of media power brokers, craving the sweet taste of power associated with this inner circle. Joe watched Carson's transformation through concerned eyes. He quickly discerned that for Carson, the allure of power was more intoxicating than the strongest whiskey behind the bar. Joe quietly hung a sign next to Carson's favorite stool, and the subtlety of the message became an ever-present reminder of the crooked paths on

Carson's journey. Each time Carson would climb onto his favorite stool, his eyes would focus on the framed quote on the wall: "*With great power comes great responsibility. Uncle Ben, by way of Voltaire.*" It was this framed quote Carson symbolically destroyed while attempting to silence his phone against the wall. The shattered words were scattered on the floor like the broken pieces of Carson's reputation.

It wasn't until the story broke that life for Carson took a dramatic and costly turn for the worse. At 34, Carson Stewart was at the top of his game as lead political columnist for *America Today*. With a nationally syndicated column, millions interpreted Carson's words each week as a primer for public perception. A politician's career could be boosted or destroyed depending on the angle of Carson's journalistic weaponry. As a 19th century robber barron once quipped, "I never pick fights with people who purchase ink by the barrel." At the height of Carson's career, pen and ink were his weapon of choice, and he wielded them with abandon.

The pressure to remain at the top, however, was daunting for Carson. To deal with the anxiety of creating the next great column, Carson did what he did best—he drank. Drinking since age sixteen to cope with the death of his mother, Carson found the numbing effects of a bottle of whiskey far outweighed the throbbing nausea of the pile-driving hangover sure to follow. Raised as an army brat and moving every few years, Carson was convinced that isolation was his closest companion. Why make friends when you had to leave them behind? His father, a Brigadier General, was known to his only son as simply, "The General." His only consistent friend was his mother, who he discovered was cheating on his father when she was killed in a car crash alongside another man. The betrayal in his life ran deep; both by the government that kept his father from him, and by the only woman in his life he trusted. Carson discovered, early, that drinking numbed the shame he felt. But it was ultimately no match for the toxic pain that lingered like shrapnel from a bad press review. Ironically, his drinking became the weapon that wrote the story of his own catastrophic public collapse.

After one evening of drinking, Carson found himself staring down the cardinal rule for a nationally syndicated columnist. In the dreaded position of missing a deadline for the paper, and in a sheer state of panic, Carson stepped over the journalistic line. With a few strokes of the keyboard, Carson ran a quick search on the Internet until he found what he needed. A few cut-and-paste edits later, the deadline was met and Carson submitted his first fully fabricated, largely plagiarized column.

The amount of time required to reveal the fabricated story was remarkable even for the national press. The media's willingness to turn on one of its own was fueled by the simmering trail of enemies made everywhere Carson ventured. Carson lived his life with the same abandon as he wrote—full throttle. His life philosophy was simple: *Trust no one but yourself, everyone is a liar*, and *women only want to hurt men*. This personal mantra alone was enough to alienate the majority of contacts in any room he entered. Combined with his recurrent episodes of drinking, there were no survivors.

A few knew Carson at a surface level, but only Joe could penetrate his brash exterior and read the tragic story of his life. Undeterred by Carson's cynical outlook on the world, Joe knew that the only hope for Carson was for Carson to find hope in himself. Like Hemingway, Twain, Fitzgerald, and so many brilliant writers in history who suffered great mental anguish and even depression, Joe knew that what didn't kill Carson made him stronger and fueled the creative engine. The interplay between Carson's flawed past, his impenetrable presence, and his no-holds-barred attitude made him an exquisite writer. For many, this was the paradox of Carson Stewart.

Carson's head remained cradled in his arms as he agonized over the throbbing pain he felt behind his eyes. He knew if he raised his head, the daylight from the small front windows would penetrate the far reaches of his brain, illuminating the discomfort he was experiencing.

"You need to drink your water if you are going to face the day," came the familiar voice of Joe from the far side of the bar.

In a less-than-audible voice, Carson responded, "Who said I wanted to face the day?"

The
CALL

The ringing was a bit of a surprise, considering Carson's phone lay in pieces, splayed across the old wooden floor of the pub. After a couple of rings, the sound was replaced by muffled voices engaged in light chatter. Joe suddenly appeared and stood over Carson, who still had his head in his arms, face down on the bar.

"Someone wants you pretty badly to track you down through me," Joe said in a matter-of-fact tone.

"Not interested." Carson mumbled.

"Says his name is Brian Palmer," Joe replied. "He told me to tell you he is your last friend in the business, and you need to take his call."

Hearing those words, Carson made the first attempt to raise his head in over two hours. Eyes still closed to avoid the daylight, he held out his hand, suggesting he wanted Joe's phone. Joe placed the phone in Carson's palm and gently lifted it to his ear.

"What?" the guttural response was Carson's first full-strength word in hours.

"Carson, you need to get your butt off that stool and get cleaned up. I have a job for you," Brian said in a firm voice.

"Haven't you heard the news, Brian? I'm radioactive. No one is going to touch me. Why would *Common-Perspective.com* want to give me a job?" Carson challenged, emphasizing the dot com with a slight sarcasm.

"Technically, it's not a full-time job. I have a spec gig I want you to do. It will get you off that stool," said Brian.

"But I like my stool," Carson muttered, as he gently opened his eyes.

"Speaking as your last friend on the planet, I wouldn't be too picky," Brian exclaimed.

"Joe's my friend," Carson replied, evoking a raised eyebrow from Joe upon hearing his name.

"Great, but until Joe offers you a writing gig, you need to get cleaned up and meet me in two hours for lunch at Madison Square Park. No excuses," Brian added in an authoritative tone of voice.

"Okay, okay; no need to shout," Carson groaned as he held the cell phone several inches from his head. "I will be there. Can't guarantee a clean shirt, but I will be there."

Joe's mustache turned up slightly as a relieved grin elevated his massive beard. Carson muttered to himself, "Great, the only job I can get is with an overrated blog," as he buried his face deep into his hands. Standing directly in front of Carson, Joe pushed the glass of water and painkiller toward him, while simultaneously removing the glass of whiskey. Peering through the cracks in his fingers Carson proclaimed, "It will take more than a glass of water to get me off this barstool," as he reached for the pill. With a wry smile, Joe turned and walked away without saying a word.

The City was fully awake, and the smells and sounds permeated Carson's head, wreaking a new kind of havoc. He stumbled the few blocks to the Greenwich Village apartment he had rented since college. Rent control meant infrequent maintenance, and turning the key in the stubborn lock required more strength than just getting through his door. Once inside, he began peeling off the clothes he hadn't changed in three days. Walking naked through his apartment, he carefully stepped into the claw foot tub for his first shower in several days. A twist of the original brass knob, and he stood perfectly still as the temperamental flow of hot and cold water ran over his head. He rested his arms, fully extended, on the wall in front of him. After several minutes in the same posture, Carson could begin to feel the blood flowing through his body once again.

Stepping out of the shower, he picked up the closest resemblance to a clean towel within his reach. Wiping the mirror, he was alarmed by the face staring back at him. Assessing several days of beard growth and gritty teeth, he was most startled by the emptiness in the eyes locked in his gaze.

Dripping with water, Carson stood while a pool collected at his feet and, for the first time, stared deeply into the eyes looking back at him. There was something missing, something just not right. He blinked several times to clear his thoughts and bring himself back to what he considered reality. The fog in Carson's head was as thick and heavy as a midsummer rain in the City. Yet, through the haze, Carson couldn't help but recall Joe reciting the poet William Blake: *This life's dim windows of the soul distorts the heavens from pole to pole and leads you to believe a lie when you see with, not through, the eye.*

Carson remembered Joe ruminating before one of his huge interviews, challenging him to see life *through* his eyes and not merely *with* his eyes. For that brief moment, Carson could sense an inner voice lobbying to shout the truth. As quickly as the voice rose into his throat, Carson silenced it.

Managing to find his last clean shirt, Carson got dressed and headed out to hail a cab. He glanced down at his "uniform," which consisted of blue jeans, an untucked white button-down, his favorite blue blazer, and slip-on loafers that kept him from bending over to tie his shoes. He pulled his black Ray-Ban sunglasses down to protect his still-sensitive eyes from the afternoon sun. The seven steps in front of his brownstone apartment proved less challenging on the way down. Once street level, a quick turn down the block to 6th Street allowed Carson to stretch his legs for the first time in days.

"Madison Square Park," Carson told the cabbie as he leaned back into the seat. With the window open, he felt the cooling breeze wash over his face. The peaceful moment was soon shattered, bringing Carson quickly back to reality as the small digital screen attached to the back of the seat in front of him played a loop of local news. In the short ride to the park, Carson came face to face with the cold hard truth Joe had been protecting him from for the last few days. The report was brief and to the point, "Local journalist fired for plagiarism." In a flash, the rear seat of the cab began closing in on Carson with more force than an industrial car crusher. Madison Square Park couldn't arrive quickly enough.

Exiting the cab in front of the historic Flatiron Building on 23rd and 5th, Carson entered the park from the south side. It wasn't long before he spotted Brian sitting on a bench near the Southern Fountain. Brian did not have to explain what he had in mind for lunch. On several occasions, the two of them met at the *Shake Shack* in the park to talk shop over a burger. The site was both secluded and convenient, given that Brian had an office in Midtown. Today, the private setting was necessary, considering the added attention Carson had received over the last several weeks.

Brian stood to meet Carson with an extended hand. "Carson, how you holding up my friend? At least it looks like you found a clean shirt," he smiled.

"Feeling like road kill after that cab ride," Carson said, while trying his best to manage a smile.

"Let's grab a burger. A cold shake will scrape you off the pavement," Brian grinned as he began walking toward the smell of grilled burgers.

In spite of its seclusion, there was a perpetual line for this burger stand. Today was no exception. As the two waited, Carson kept his dark glasses on to avoid eye contact with anyone else in line. Noticing his discomfort, Brian worked to keep the conversation on the light side. "How is Amy?" Brian asked, inquiring about the only steady girlfriend Carson had in years.

"Sore subject." Carson responded, fixing his gaze on the person in front of him.

"Sorry to hear. I liked her," Brian offered.

"Yeah, well she said the stress of all the negative press was more than she signed up for," Carson said, with slight disdain in his voice. "Guessing road kill wasn't on her menu." Carson's slightly elevated tone caused the girl in front of him to stiffly turn and find the source of the dead animal comment. "Worked out, actually. She was getting on my nerves," Carson continued, emphasizing the last few words as he met the gaze of the women in front of him.

"At least you haven't let it ruin your Prince Charming personality," Brian teased, evoking a classic New Yorker smirk of agreement from the lady who was now clearly part of their conversation. Before stepping up to the window to order, she managed to get in a parting shot.

"Schmuck, doesn't surprise me she left you," she said in a Yiddish accent, dripping with the full measure of sarcasm she intended. Her comment hit Carson like another-sucker punch in what felt like an 18-rounder with Muhammad Ali. Brian knew Carson had been hurt by Amy's departure, and this interaction did not help. He decided to let the topic drop for now. Knowing Carson's trouble with maintaining a relationship, Brian was really not surprised to hear the news.

People from all walks of life inhabited the flimsy green tables scattered like a checkerboard throughout the City's park. From stockbrokers to tourists, the burger joint frequently filled to capacity, and today it was packed. Finding a table along the edge of the crushed granite pathway closest to Broadway, the two commanded one of the last remaining tables. Finally, they were able to relax for just a brief moment in the middle of a city that never relaxed.

"I know this has been rough on you." Brian began, salting his French fries and adjusting his chair.

"Your little blog hasn't shown any mercy," Carson quickly interjected, peeling back the wrapping around his burger as he prepared for his first bite.

"Well, you've managed to piss a few people off over the years, Carson, and folks at that 'little blog,' as you put it, have a very long memory. You do know we have a national audience, we're not just a blog," Brian continued.

"It was just business, Brian," Carson looked away, as his voice trailed off. "It was nothing personal."

"Some took it personally, I'm afraid," Brian replied. "You know as well as I do, that this industry is long on memory and short on forgiveness."

"Then why are we talking?" Carson asked cautiously.

"We've known each other since college. You were a jerk then and still one today. If you don't believe me, ask the lady in line," Brian began with a smirk, lightening his tone. "But I have always held out hope that deep inside you was a good person looking to find his way out."

"When did you become Dr. Phil?" Carson looked up from his shake and searched Brian's eyes for any sign of insincerity. In college Brian was always a step away from Carson, looking up to him as a mentor in their last years of school. As they entered the workforce, it was Carson who helped Brian land his first intern gig at the then-start-up blog where he worked his way up to editor of the fast-growing online news outlet. Brian had modeled the early part of his career after the white-hot trajectory that was Carson's career path—that is, until Carson's integrity began to slip. Over the past few years, the two had slowly drifted to opposite sides of a wide ethical chasm, carved by the flow of alcohol. But, Brian never gave up on the person who so generously gave of himself in their early years, and he was the first to offer help when Carson needed it the most.

Brian's calm gaze offered reassurance. "Look, I was offended by what you did as much as anyone in the business. You screwed up and deserve the natural consequences of violating your ethics. I do, however, believe in second chances," Brian said, thoughtfully. "Lord knows, I've received my fair share. You need to know there is more to life than the bottom of a bottle. In fact, as crazy as this may sound to you, I believe we are put here for a purpose. I just thought you might be interested in a shot at redemption, and a little help figuring out what your purpose is in all of this."

The words of his only remaining friend in the business washed over Carson as he stared back at Brian through his dark sunglasses. Even the Ray-Bans could not conceal the slight moisture in his eyes. Deep inside, he knew there was more to life, but he had always felt unworthy of anything more. The shame of his past burned a hole inside him—a hole that, up to this point, had been impossible to fill. Even the temporary peace and numbness courtesy of a bottle of whiskey could not fill the void.

"I'm not sure I am redeemable, old friend," Carson began, his voice hinting at sudden interest. "What do you have in mind?"

Brian leaned back slightly in his chair and began, "I want to run a series on Clara Becker, a congresswomen from Texas. Seems she has unequaled longevity maintaining the highest approval rating in Congress. There is an important story here, and I want you to write it."

"I know of her," Carson said, his journalistic cynicism returning. "No one can be that good for that long. Texas is too big for her to be the lone star in the Lone Star State." Brian leaned over the table, removing his sunglasses to lock eyes with Carson. In a deliberate way, he peered directly through the dark Ray-Bans Carson was wearing.

"Carson, you need this story. You need to see there is good in people and this is a chance to write something that isn't ultimately intended to destroy your adversary." Brian sat back again and added, "The assignment is a simple 10,000-word spec gig. I can give you an advance and cover your expenses out of my section budget to get you started. The piece will run in three months. You'll get paid based on the click-through rate. If the traffic is worthy then we will do a follow up story. That gives you time to do your research and allows more time for your current story to fade." Carson knew his old friend was risking his career by putting him on this story. Should this assignment go wrong, the internal backlash would bankrupt Brian's reputation.

Uncomfortable without a barrier hiding his emotion, Carson looked down, took the last slurp of his shake, and said, "You're right about one thing, this shake is scraping me up from the road kill position. I appreciate the opportunity, Brian." For Brian, this was the closest thing to a thank you he had ever heard from Carson.

"You're welcome, Carson." Brian exclaimed, realizing they had just exchanged their first honest dialogue in a decade.

We both know the real story is what gets clicks in today's market," Carson said, challenging his gaze.

Brian never blinked as he replied, "You get one shot at getting this right. If you go digging for a story on Clara that is not there, you will be done. Heck, we will both be done. The two of us won't be able to write obits for the *Duncan Banner* if you screw this up."

Carson pushed his chair back and gathered his trash from the table. "You will get your story—the full story, on time I might add," Carson said with a tone of reassurance. "I am looking forward to it."

Brian extended his hand. "I believe in you, old friend. I will have the office email over the details," he added, as he turned and strode toward the car waiting for him.

Carson decided to walk back to his place from the park. The longer Carson walked, the greater the pressure began to build. He could only think of one thing by the time he had covered only five blocks—the location of the nearest bar. "Just one drink to calm my nerves," was the thought that ran through his mind as he searched the city streets. His plan was to go home and pack for D.C., fueled by one glass of liquid courage. But this was the fatal flaw in most of Carson's plans—there was no such thing as one drink. The flight to D.C. would need to wait, for tonight there would be more than one drink and yet another missed opportunity to do the right thing.

The
INTERVIEW

Having spent 24 hours blacked out, Carson spent most of the early morning hours of the following day scanning the Internet and conducting preliminary research on Congresswoman Clara Becker. He was still hungover and wearing the same clothes from his lunch with Brian. Carson sat in the one chair in his apartment; a cup of instant coffee in one hand while balancing his laptop on his shaky legs. He couldn't discern if the pounding in his head was from the hangover or the incessant construction work on the city streets. This morning, it happened to be both.

Information on the congresswoman was not difficult to come by, given her tenure in Congress. As a six-term Republican member of the House of Representatives, Clara Becker was one of the senior members of Congress. Chairing the House Ways and Means Committee, the congresswoman was one of the most powerful individuals on the Hill.

In the Moleskine journal that never left his side, Carson recorded pages of basic data. Turning the page, he wrote at the top, "People to interview." Carson tapped his pen on the page several times as he considered names to record. Within a few seconds, the pages were pockmarked from the nervous pen taps, yet they were still blank. Carson's face flushed with shame, as he comprehended the struggle he would face putting his career back on track. The big question of the day: "Who would take his call?"

Sitting in his chair, the streetlights illuminating the living room cast a shadow over the page in his journal. Carson's thoughts quickly deteriorated, shifting the blame to Brian for putting him in the situation. "What was I thinking?" he asked himself, as he sat motionless, glaring into space. Within a matter of moments, Carson's victim mentality had him convinced he was being set up to fail. Under his current circumstances, finding an interviewee on the Hill who hadn't read about his tarnished career seemed hopeless.

Succumbing to a mild depression, Carson considered avoiding the daunting task before him by texting Brian and declining his offer. Reaching for his phone, he realized it was in multiple pieces on the floor at *Joe's Place*. Hopelessness washed over Carson as he heaved his weight out of the chair to find a bottle of anything in the apartment. Looking at his watch, he calculated the time until he needed to catch the shuttle flight to D.C. Startled by the hour, he decided to pack a bag instead, and head straight to La Guardia Airport. Certainly, a bar there would be able to accommodate his needs.

Once through security, Carson made his way to the first place that looked open for business. While most people standing in line at this hour were placing orders for their morning coffee and breakfast sandwich, Carson had another form of nourishment in mind. Realizing his choice was limited to a cold beer, Carson settled for a Bud Light along with an egg, bacon, and cheese biscuit. "Brian better have set me up with a real drink," he thought, as he boarded his flight.

To sweeten the deal for Carson, Brian was generous enough to cover first class travel on his research trips. Once settled on board for the short flight to Reagan Airport, he quickly requested a whiskey neat from the flight attendant. Settling back into his seat, Carson pulled his journal from his well-worn leather bag. Reviewing his notes, he recognized his best hope for getting the story was to secure an interview directly with the congresswoman. To pull that off, he decided to cash in his last favor from within the Beltway.

Carson jotted down a reminder to call Ross Horner once he landed. Ross was possibly the only person on earth who owed Carson a favor. As Chief of Staff for a second-term congressman from the South, Ross had once enticed Carson to write a column on the positive work the congressman was doing in his home state. The timeliness of the column fueled an easy re-election campaign for Ross and the legislator. Celebrating the victory, Ross called Carson to thank him and remarked, "If you ever need a favor, just call." Carson was a man who desperately needed a favor, and he planned on finding Ross and reminding him of his timeless offer.

As the American Airlines 737 made its final approach, the landing pattern afforded the passengers on the left side of the plane a magnificent view of the Capitol. For all his failings, Carson's heart still pounded like a racehorse as he caught his first, splendorous glimpse of the nation's Capitol.

Once the wheels touched the ground, Carson located the disposable phone he'd purchased in the airport and turned to a page in the back of his journal where several names and numbers were written in a form of shorthand code. The cache of information contained in Carson's journal would be devastating in the wrong hands. In college, he created shorthand that only he could decipher in the event he was ever separated from his journal.

Carson wasted no time typing out a text message. *"Ross, it's Carson Stewart. Need to collect on the favor you owe. Meet me at the Willard for drinks. 2:00 p.m."*

Within a few moments, Carson received a terse reply: *"Surprised to hear from you. Can only spare a few minutes. 2:00 p.m. sharp."*

And with that, Carson was back in the game.

Entering the lobby of the historic hotel, Carson made a direct path to the bar. Walking through the Willard was like traversing the history of politics. Not only had every president for the last century stayed at the Willard, the National Press Club was founded here in 1908. Carson was hoping to make a little history of his own.

At 2:00 p.m. sharp, Ross arrived while Carson was well into his third whiskey. "What will you have?" Carson asked while Ross looked furtively around the room like a fugitive desiring anonymity. "None for me," Ross waved him off. "As I said in my text, I am a bit surprised you showed your face in town. So, what can I help you with?" Ross continued, getting straight to the point.

"I'm doing some research." Carson replied, as he set down his glass and pushed it away. "Need your help in setting up an interview."

"With whom?" Ross hesitated.

"Clara Becker from Texas," Carson offered as he opened his notebook, his pen poised to take notes.

"You're kidding, right?" Ross said sarcastically, assessing the hubris of Carson's request.

"Dead serious." Carson said with the most confident, sober-sounding voice he could muster. Ross noted the underlying insecurity in Carson's bold ask.

"Look Carson, I owe you a favor and I will make good on it. But, what you are asking I am not sure I can deliver. You might as well be asking for an interview with the President," Ross said, while scrolling through his contacts. "The best I could do is a contact in Ms. Becker's media office," he offered.

"Heck, Ross, I can pull that name off the Internet. I need an interview not a brush-off," Carson sat up straight, his voice gaining more force. Ross needed time to assess the political collateral damage this request might cost his office.

"Let me work on it and get back to you," Ross said as he slowly got up. "Keep your phone close. I will have something for you in a couple of hours." He turned and walked away from Carson, signaling his few minutes were up and this session was closed.

Carson reached for his unfinished drink and made a note in his journal where the contacts should have gone: "No one with this much power can be this good. What is the real story?" He underlined the last question several times for added impact. By the time Carson looked up, a crowd of suits from the Hill had engulfed the bar, making him increasingly uneasy. It was this uneasiness that sent a shiver down Carson's spine as he became acutely aware of the collective judgment that had been heaped upon him. Less than a year ago, Carson would have ruled this room of power brokers. Today, they were the judge and jury, applying twice the weight and pressure than the words that used to flow from his pen. Seconds felt like hours as the suffocating crush of judgmental stares pierced his heart.

Every fiber in Carson's body began to recoil like a rattlesnake ready to strike. In his mind, Carson was preparing a vicious verbal counterattack to his surrounding prey. Remembering Brian's quip about writing obits in *Duncan*, he thought it best to avoid the viral YouTube scene he would have created. He quickly slipped out of the historic bar as discreetly as possible, stepping outside to clear his head. Emerging onto Pennsylvania Avenue, Carson turned right and headed toward the White House. At this time of day, the streets were teeming with a mix of government employees and tourists. Heading north on 14th Street, he closed the distance between the bar and his favorite park space in the city.

Once settled on a park bench, he took in the view of the North Lawn of the White House, a tourist's favorite picture spot. Carson began to review his notes while periodically glancing at the vibrant passersby. The north side was always bustling with activity. On any given day, one could witness a protest, a prayer vigil, a tour group, and a lesson on border security. For years, Carson's exclusive press credentials gave him direct access and authority to report on the events, the people, and the power behind the black iron fence at 1600 Pennsylvania Avenue. The burning desire to be restored to the game began to consume Carson's every thought. "WHATEVER IT TAKES!" was the next entry Carson printed in his journal using all capital letters. *And I mean WHATEVER,* he thought as he closed his journal, crossed his arms, and waited to hear from Ross.

As Carson waited, his mind drifted to a lively debate he once had with Joe about politicians in D.C. Joe had written a paper in college on Lord Acton, and it was one of the few times Carson had a leg up on Joe, having quoted Acton many times in his articles. "Power tends to corrupt and absolute power corrupts absolutely," Carson said, quoting Lord Acton's most famous line. Carson had continued, "And, Acton went on to say, 'Great men are almost always bad men' which is why my 2nd Life Rule is, 'Don't trust anyone.'"

Carson smiled as he recalled Joe's response, "Even when bad men fall—and we all fall from time to time—shouldn't we pick them up, forgive them, and set them on a path to be great men?" Carson always appreciated Joe's simple wisdom, but staring at the White House today, he was convinced his 2nd Life Rule was truer than ever; "Don't trust anyone—even Clara Becker."

The
INSIDER

The light vibration of his phone broke Carson's reflective trance. Without looking at the number, he raised the device to his ear. "What do you have for me, Ross?"

The tone of Ross's voice dripped with distaste, clearly uncomfortable with what he was about to do.

"Becker's office is out, so I did one better for you."

"Great, what do you have?" responded Carson, with a slight uptick in his voice.

"Congressman Ryan Burr is the person to interview if you want the real story on Becker," explained Ross. "His communications guy, Malcolm Claire, has agreed to a full access interview with Burr."

With the phone tucked into the fold of Carson's neck, he quickly recorded notes into his journal. "How do I connect with Claire?" Carson asked, prepared to write down a number to call.

"You don't. He will reach out to you. I gave him this number," Ross replied.

"When should I expect a call?" asked Carson, somewhat disappointed he didn't connect him directly to Clara's office. "Just stay close to the phone," Ross said. "And Carson, we are done. Don't call me again." With that, Ross hung up the phone.

Slipping the phone in his jacket pocket, Carson began to write in his journal. His first thought was, "Who is Ryan Burr?" Having spent considerable time in D.C., Carson knew most of the players in the city. Ryan Burr was a bit of a mystery to Carson, as he had never written a story on the congressman. A wash of anxiety rushed over him as he considered the possibility that Ross gave him a dud interview just to clear the debt.

Determined to make the best of what he had before him, Carson gathered himself and looked for a place nearby he could conduct his research. Just a few blocks away, Carson recalled a pub on 1st Street with free WiFi that could serve as a temporary office. Several questions flooded Carson's mind as he walked briskly towards 1st, never looking up from his journal as he studied his notes.

While standing at the crosswalk at H and 16th Street, the phone in Carson's pocket began to vibrate. Reaching in his pocket, he pulled out the phone and noted the blocked number recorded on the screen. With no hesitation, he pressed the green button and said, "Carson here."

The voice on the other end boomed, "Carson, my friend, this is Malcolm Claire. I understand you are looking for an interview."

Carson's reflexes took over as he responded, "You are correct, as long we are both talking about Congressman Burr."

Malcolm chucked as he responded, "I handle communications for Congressman Burr. He is extremely busy, but Ross insisted it would be worth our time to grant you a quick interview. I can get you a solid hour between engagements tomorrow if you can be in New York City. He has a fundraiser dinner in Midtown. We can meet in his suite prior to an event he is hosting at the Waldorf Hotel. Be in the lobby at 4:45 sharp. Our men will find you and bring you up."

Carson was writing the details in his journal as he spoke up, "I can make that work, thank you. An hour will be plenty of time." He scribbled the instructions furiously, not missing a detail.

"Great, see you at the Waldorf tomorrow," Malcolm responded and the conversation was over.

Carson's head was still buried in his notebook as he continued to the pub. Suddenly, Carson's heart stopped at the blaring of a high-pitched car horn. In total shock, he looked up to see the front grill of a Lincoln Town Car just inches from his body. The driver in the car was expressing his thoughts for Carson's lack of attention with the same hand gestures as the cabbies in New York. His heart still racing, Carson collected his thoughts and hustled to the opposite side of the street, a bit more aware of his surroundings.

Once standing on the north side of H Street, Carson paused to allow his breathing to return to normal. Still dazed by the near miss, Carson could feel his insides tighten up from the sudden jolt of adrenaline that had rushed through his body. Clutching his journal tighter, he quickly covered the last few blocks, his mind completely consumed with getting a drink to calm his nerves.

Once settled in a small booth towards the back of the pub, Carson ordered his usual drink, and pulled out his laptop to connect to WiFi. Flipping through the pages of his journal, he came to the name Malcolm Claire. Typing the name into Google revealed a limited, vague search result. Clicking on the one promising link opened a single page website with the following information.

Malcolm Claire
Public Relations
New York City, New York

Towards the bottom of the page was a single word, "Contact," that was underlined with a hyperlink. Clicking on the word, revealed what appeared to be a standard fill-in-the-blank information request page.

Opening a separate window in his browser, Carson expanded his search on Malcolm. Little-to-no information existed, which immediately raised a series of questions in Carson's mind. There was only one place to go for more information, and only one person he trusted with his search: Joe.

Back in the City, Carson climbed into the back of the hired black SUV. "Midtown, 42nd and 5th," Carson said as he settled in. Removing his phone from his bag, he dialed Joe's number, one of the few he had memorized.

The familiar voice on the other end boomed out, "Go for Joe!"

"Joe, it's Carson. Heading your way. Need some information on a guy named Malcolm Claire. I think he's some kind of PR guy in the City," Carson explained, staring out the side window at the city skyline in the distance.

"I will make some calls and have something for you later tonight. You in the City?" Joe asked.

"Just landed. Have a couple of errands to run. Be by later. Thanks, Joe," Carson said as he hung up the phone, knowing Joe wasn't a goodbye kind of guy.

The SUV pulled to the side of the curb to let Carson out. "Drop my bag at *Joe's Place* located at 7th and Christopher in the Village. Let him know it's mine and I will be by later to get it," Carson explained to the driver. Crossing the street, Carson headed for the New York Public Library. The steps of the library were dotted with people, mostly tourists, enjoying the pleasant afternoon in the City.

Climbing the first tier of steps next to the massive carved crouching lion, Carson spotted the person he was meeting. Sitting in the classic green folding chair with his back to the lion was Brian Palmer, carefully studying the email on his phone. "Don't you ever have meetings in your office?" Carson asked as he pulled up one of the few remaining green chairs.

"The City is too perfect today to waste it inside. What do you have for me?" Brian asked.

Carson removed his journal and responded while flipping pages, "What can you tell me about Ryan Burr, congressman from New York?"

"Well-liked in the City and very ambitious. Why do you ask?" Brian replied, with a slight tone of curiosity.

"Seems my only way to Clara Becker is through Burr," Carson said in a very matter-of-fact way.

"I will have some information emailed over to you today," Brian responded. "Now, let's grab some lunch." The two descended the steps to find a place to eat. Standing at the corner, Brian couldn't help but notice the strong odor of alcohol on Carson's breath. "You sleep in a bar last night?" Brian asked, with a bit of a chuckle.

"Had a near-death experience and needed a few drinks to calm my nerves, that's all," Carson explained.

"You keep drinking at your current pace and you're certain to have another near-death experience sooner rather than later," Brian responded, trying to keep the conversation light.

Timing the light perfectly, Brian stepped into the street while Carson hesitated ever so slightly, whispering softly to himself, "I know."

Later that afternoon, Carson pushed through the dark oak door at *Joe's Place*. The establishment was beginning to show signs of life with a group of regulars already crowded up to the bar. Spotting Carson, Joe pulled a clean glass from under the bar, poured two fingers of whiskey, and placed it in front of the stool at the far end. Carson pushed the stool to one side, placed his elbows on the bar top, and leaned in to speak to Joe. "Find anything?" he asked in a soft tone. Joe pulled a large envelope from under the bar and placed it in front of Carson.

"I found out plenty," Joe said. "Seems Malcolm is some kind of high profile fixer. He has a list of impressive power clients all over the world." Joe wiped down the bar top as he spoke, mostly out of nervous habit.

"What is he trying to fix with Burr?" Carson asked, while picking up the envelope in front of him.

"According to my sources, Malcolm has scaled up his practice and is now helping Burr become President." Carson stopped mid-motion, looking up at Joe with a blank expression on his face. The plot to this story was beginning to thicken faster than the beard on Joe's face.

Setting the envelope down, Carson reached into his bag to pull out his journal and record the latest revelation. As he was writing, without looking up he asked, "What's in the envelope?"

"Not sure. About an hour after I made some calls on Malcolm and Burr, a bike messenger dropped this off with a note to give it to you. Thought it might be from Brian," Joe explained.

"That's odd. I just had lunch with Brian and he didn't say anything about a delivery." Carson shrugged.

Picking up the envelope, Carson ripped off the top and poured the contents onto the bar. It contained an invitation to the Waldorf dinner, a note card, and a black flip phone. The note read, "Use this phone once you get to the hotel. The number is preprogrammed. MC."

Carson had more questions than answers, including how Malcolm knew where to find him and why he would need what he assumed was a secured line. "What do you make of this, Joe?" Carson asked.

"It would appear Malcolm Burr, aka 'the Fixer,' is well-connected. My advice, tread very carefully," Joe said as he flipped a white towel over his shoulder.

Still holding the phone in his hands, Carson glanced at the drink in front of him. The words from his conversation with Brian started bouncing around in his head. Grabbing his bag, Carson tossed the contents of the envelope into the side pocket, placing the phone in his jacket. As he headed for the front door, Joe yelled out, "You didn't finish your drink!"

"Not thirsty," Carson replied, never breaking stride.

Joe stopped in his tracks and watched as the last rays of light closed on Carson as he disappeared through the door. "Finally," Joe whispered under his breath.

The
WALDORF

The line of limos was twenty deep on Park Avenue in front of the historic hotel. Arriving fashionably early was an art form in the City. Carson pulled the cuffs on the freshly pressed shirt out of his jacket to reveal just the right amount of sleeve. As he entered the grand lobby of the hotel through the Park Avenue entrance, the wash of history was not lost on him. Climbing the steps to the main level revealed the magnificent artwork on the lobby floor.

Heading forward through the throng of perfectly dressed guests, Carson made his way towards the main lobby. As he was walking towards the landmark clock, two men came alongside him. "Mr. Stewart, if you will follow us, the congressman is waiting," said the gentleman to Carson's right. Extending his hand towards the elevators, the other man placed his right hand on Carson's shoulder to guide him along.

Over the years, Carson had interviewed hundreds of people in high-ranking positions. For some reason, tonight felt different. Facing the front of the elevator behind the dark-suited security detail, Carson's mind raced to process the events. The doors opened to the corridor leading to the Churchill Suite.

Once inside the dark paneled room, Carson took in its exquisite details. From the baby grand piano to the view of the City, everything was pristine. Seated behind the wooden desk, the congressman's personal assistant poured over the agenda for the evening. Additional staff busily studied their phones for the latest details regarding tonight's dinner.

Standing to greet him as he entered the room was Congressman Ryan Burr. "You must be Carson Stewart. Nice to meet you. I am Ryan Burr." Carson extended his hand and was met with the firm, almost bone-crushing grip of the congressman.

"Nice to meet you, sir," Carson said.

"Please, call me Ryan."

"Very well," Carson replied.

Ryan Burr was a slender man of average height. A well-tailored blue, pinstriped suit with a custom blue tie was the perfect choice for tonight's event. Every detail about Ryan Burr was impeccable. A native of New York, Ryan's family dated back to the beginning of the nation.

Ryan sat on the edge of the overstuffed sofa while Carson placed his bag down and took a seat, pulling up a red and white striped chair. Just as they were getting settled, a gentleman entered from an adjoining room. Extending his hand, he approached Carson and said in a booming voice, "Malcolm Claire—glad you could make it." Carson began to rise out of his chair to shake hands with Malcolm when he was waved back. "Stay seated, son, time is short. Let's get started." Malcolm took a step closer. "I understand you are doing a piece on Clara Becker," Malcolm continued. "Ryan and Clara have worked together for several years. We should be able to help you out."

In what appeared to be a well-timed tag team, Ryan spoke almost on queue, "Malcolm, why don't you give Carson and me a few minutes alone." With those words, Malcolm motioned for the security detail and the staff to follow him out of the room, leaving Carson and the congressman alone.

"I wanted for us to have some privacy," Ryan offered, as he stood and walked over to the cart containing a complete assortment of beverages. "Pour you a drink? Whiskey, is it?" Ryan asked as he picked up a glass.

"Water if you have it," Carson responded, not believing those words came out of his mouth.

"Carson, can I trust you?" asked Ryan as he poured water into a glass for Carson.

"Seems like a fair question given recent events," Carson replied. "Yes, you can trust me."

"Good," Ryan replied as he handed the glass of water to Carson. "I want to help you get back in the game, but I need your help in the process," Ryan said as he sat back down on the sofa.

"What kind of help?" Carson asked, wary but interested.

"I have it on good authority that Clara Becker is trying to sell government secrets to our enemies," Ryan lowered his voice and leaned forward for effect. Carson placed his drink on the table and reached for his journal.

"What type of secrets?" Carson asked.

"Let's just say the kind that would get people killed if they got out," Ryan responded as he settled back into the sofa and took a long sip of his drink.

"And why would the highest-ranking member of Congress holding a spotless record want to sell government secrets?" Carson asked, feeling the old energy beginning to re-enter his body.

"Power, of course," Ryan replied without missing a beat.

"If you have this information, why work with me?" Carson asked. "You could go to the DOJ and have her investigated."

"Investigations take too long. This is going to require a little push, and that is where you come in," Ryan said. "I will give you the details of what is happening. You create the awareness, which will prod the DOJ into fast-tracking an investigation." Ryan got up from the sofa to pace the room. "We both get what we want," Ryan added, slowing up a bit. "Just one thing—my name can't be attached to this story in any possible way." Carson looked up from his journal.

"A no-name source always draws attention," Carson said.

"I know; you will figure that out. Do we have a deal?" Ryan said as he made his way back to Carson's side and extended his hand to shake.

Carson rose out of his chair and reached out to shake the Congressman's hand. "Deal."

"Great. Malcolm will handle much of the communication flow. Keep the phone we gave you close. He will be in contact," Ryan stated. "I do need to run. Donors are waiting. Please, feel free to order room service and have dinner in the suite. You can't beat the views of the City," Ryan offered as he buttoned his jacket and headed for the door. A swarm of staff greeted him in the hall to escort him to the ballroom, where four hundred donors awaited his entrance.

Carson sat back down into the chair to process what just happened. His mind was racing, but for the first time in several weeks he was able to systematically sort through the information. In his journal he made a note. *What does Burr gain from Becker going down?* Closing his notebook, Carson gathered his bag and headed for the door.

"Do you think he will do it?" Ryan Burr asked Malcolm as they entered the elevator.

"He'll do it. He is addicted to the game the same he is to whiskey. He wants back in and this story is his ticket," Malcolm said as he pushed the button for the ballroom floor.

"Timing is important on this," Ryan offered as the elevator made its way to its destination.

"I have everything under control. The story will break and give us three to four media cycles before you come in and clean things up—just in time for the nominations," Malcolm said. "Once we clear Clara out of the way, there will be nothing between us and the Presidency," he added.

"I like Clara, but nothing is getting in the way of the White House—nothing!" Ryan said, as the doors of the elevator opened to a throng of people waiting for the Congressman. On cue, he exited the elevator with extended hand, calling the first person he saw by name as he began to work the room.

Lingering behind and blending into the crowd, Malcolm watched his client make his way across the room. "Next stop, the White House," he whispered as he trailed behind him.

The
INVITATION

Fundraising was an art form for most politicians, but for Clara Becker it was a distraction. Clara preferred to spend her time lending her name to other charitable efforts. In the state of Texas, there were ample opportunities for the congresswoman to help raise awareness and much needed support for causes closest to her heart.

Sara Davis entered the office of the congresswoman. "We need to head to the airport if we are going to make our flight," Sara said as the congresswoman was finishing up the last line of a personal note.

"We will be fine, Miss Sara," Clara responded, never looking up from her desk. Signing her name, she placed the card in an envelope and handed the finished product to Sara. "Please make sure this gets dropped in the mail on our way out," Clara directed, standing to gather her jacket and bag.

As the two walked to the door, other staff members wished them a safe flight home. The two-week holiday away from the D.C. office was always a welcome break. Sara checked her phone one last time to ensure the car was waiting for the congresswoman as planned. Heading down the corridor, Clara was stopped multiple times by those wishing her a safe and happy holiday break. Over the years, the number of friends Clara Becker had made in Washington was impossible to count.

Once inside the car and settled in her seat, Clara asked the one question Sara was hoping she would forget. "Did you find someone to invite to the Ball?" Clara inquired, trying to be nonchalant. Simply called "The Ball," Clara was referring to one of the biggest charity events in Texas. The Cowboy Barons Ball focused its efforts on *Giving Cancer the Boot*, and Clara Becker had been asked to be one of the main speakers this year. Lending her name to the invitation was a sure way to guarantee that the Dallas elite would turn out in droves to support this important cause.

Hiding behind her signature aviator sunglasses, Sara glanced down at her phone, pretending to be focused on important matters. Clara shifted her body to look more directly at Sara and with a gentle smile, stared at Sara. Sara sat quietly, hoping the Congresswoman's phone would ring and save her from answering the question—a question that had been the topic of more than one conversation between the entire D.C. staff: "Will Sara finally have a date for the Ball?"

Growing up in Highland Park, the epicenter of Dallas high society, Sara was no stranger to the philanthropic social season. In her neighborhood, Sara had observed the city's movers and shakers from an early age. Her prep school education assured her admission into any Ivy League school of her choice. Having lost her father at the beginning of her first year of middle school, Sara found herself growing up much quicker than normal girls. Her father was a successful real estate developer, working projects across the country before his untimely death. Sara's mother, an attorney for a local Dallas law firm, did her best to ensure Sara's life remained as normal as was possible in their privileged neighborhood. Never remarrying, Anne devoted all she had to Sara.

At 5-foot-5, Sara's petite size was deceiving. An All-State soccer player in high school, Sara's small stature was compensated by her explosive speed and agility. In college, Sara channeled her endless energy into weekly yoga and kickboxing regimens. With a laser focus on her education, there was no time for a serious relationship during college. Not that there weren't plenty of attempts by the opposite sex. Sara was always the person who lit up the room while befriending everyone in her path. Reaching out to the alienated, she had the unique ability to make everyone believe they were part of something bigger in life.

Once Sara completed college with a B.A. in Journalism, she went on to study law at SMU in Dallas. It was during the summer of her final year in law school that Sara first came into contact with Clara Becker. Completing a summer internship for a federal judge, Sara and Clara officially met for the first time at a charity dinner hosted by the judge. For nearly an hour while listening to the judge brag about Sara, Clara finally made her way to meet the young superstar. Sara was everything Clara expected. That evening, Clara handed Sara her card and asked her to look her up should she ever decide to come to D.C. and make a difference. Clara had known there was something special about Sara Davis for some time, and their first formal meeting confirmed to Clara that Sara belonged on her staff.

Once Sara came on board, it was clear to Clara that she recognized a younger version of herself in Sara. The countless hours spent together during the last few years forged a special relationship between them. For Sara, Clara had become a valued mentor and close friend, demonstrating to Sara how to survive inside the Beltway with one's integrity intact. Sara knew that a person could ask for no better mentor in life than Congresswoman Clara Becker from the great state of Texas.

Sara could feel the weight of Clara's gaze as she awaited an answer. If she had learned one thing about the congresswoman over the years, it was that she never gave up. Relaxing her hands and phone into her lap, Sara softly responded, "No, Congresswoman—no date to the Ball."

"Well that just won't do," replied Clara in a very matter-of-fact tone of voice.

"It is quite all right, I have much to do and it wouldn't be fair to someone else," Sara tried to explain. While Clara admired Sara for her selfless ability to think of others first, she worried that Sara didn't focus enough energy on herself.

"Nonsense young lady, I can take care of myself during the fancy shindig. You, Miss Sara, need to enjoy the evening," announced Clara. "If I need to wave my wand and turn a pumpkin into your ride, I will!" Clara turned back, waving her hand in a wand-like motion, suggesting she just had the last word in the conversation.

"Yes, Congresswoman," Sara replied. Clara smiled gently, knowing Sara was fully aware how much she disliked the formality of her title. It was that sassy spark in Sara that always caused Clara to reminisce about her younger years.

"Just one quick piece of business," Sara announced as the car pulled in front of main terminal of Regan Airport.

"Yes?" Clara responded, collecting her briefcase.

"Your press briefing before the Ball includes Carson Stewart," Sara said with slight disdain in her voice. Clara hesitated before responding. "Who is Carson working for these days?"

"Seems he is credentialed with *CommonPerspective.com*, if you can believe it," Sara said, as she was gathering her things to exit the car.

As they stepped onto the walkway to enter the airport terminal, Clara turned to Sara and said softly, "Everyone deserves a second chance—even Carson Stewart."

The larger-than-life invitation reflected all that was loud, bold, and voluminous about the State of Texas. Carson held the save-the-date in one hand as he dialed Brian with his other. While it rang, Carson pressed the speaker button on his new smart phone. "Hey Carson, what's up?" Brian answered.

"Looking at my mighty-big invite along with press credentials for some sort of cattle auction in Dallas. You know anything about this?"

Brian sighed, then responded, "That would be *Cowboy Barons Ball*, one of the highlights on the social calendar of Dallas high society."

"And why I am going to this?" Carson asked without hiding his dislike for philanthropic gatherings of the elite.

"I received a package in the mail with the tickets and a request to have you credentialed for pre-Ball interviews. It seems someone worked out a deal for you to interview Clara Becker."

Carson lowered the invitation and stared at the phone sitting on the arm of his chair. "Who sent you the package?" Carson asked.

"Malcolm Claire's office sent it over via bike messenger first thing this morning. I pulled the paperwork together to get your credentials and sent it your way," Brian responded. Carson squeezed his eyes tightly shut to help redirect the pain building behind his eyes. It had been 48 hours since his last drink and the headaches were becoming more frequent. He knew this was an important moment. Six months ago, he would have been filled with excitement at the thought of a thirty-minute interview with anyone in Congress. Today, just thinking about walking into a room of his former peers was a terrifying thought.

"You still there?" came the voice through the speaker.

Carson, jolting back from his momentary paralysis, responded, "I'm here, sorry. Was just thinking."

"You can do your thinking on the plane ride to Dallas. You need to be getting packed," Brian said. "Oh, and by the way, pack your best cowboy chic outfit. You don't want to look like a tourist from out of town," Brian chuckled, wondering what cowboy chic would look like on Carson Stewart.

Carson tapped his phone to end the call and processed the unfolding events. The speed in which he found himself reentering the game was staggering. Reaching for his journal, he began to record some draft questions for Clara Becker. Partway through his first thought, he paused, and in a loud voice, proclaimed, "What the hell is cowboy chic?"

The
BALL

The high-back, velour sofa provided a natural hiding spot for Carson to nurse his large drip coffee from *Morsel's*. Situated by an expansive fireplace, he enjoyed the additional touch of warmth on this Dallas fall evening. As Carson made edits to the interview questions in his journal, a soft female voice broke the silence. "You must be Carson Stewart?"

Somewhat startled, Carson looked up from his notes right into the vivid blue eyes of Sara Davis, who happened to be holding a similar cup of coffee and was dressed in a strapless, cocktail-length sequined dress with custom cowboy boots. Carson immediately noticed that the brilliant blue sequins were no match for the sapphire depth of her eyes. Her hair, curled and hanging gently across her shoulders, lightly grazed the pearl necklace adorning her delicate collarbone—the perfect accessory for her stunning Ball attire. Entranced, Carson took a slow sip of his coffee, as the lump in his throat appeared to have cut off all the oxygen to his brain.

"Mr. Stewart, right?" Sara repeated, as she watched Carson fumble with his drink. For all his faults, Carson cleaned up well. At 6-foot-2, his lean frame still managed to show some muscle tone, despite the fact that his most frequent workouts had been limited to lifting whiskey to his lips. His thick, dark, wavy hair was slicked back with copious amounts of hair product. A rugged, tightly trimmed beard framed his strong jawline, while accenting the deep green of his eyes. "I see you found *Morsel's*," she added, trying to break his awkward silence. "I would have taken you for a latte drinker, being from New York and all."

"Hardly," Carson put his cup down. "Never confirmed mine was filled with coffee." Regaining his classic, smug, sarcastic tone, he stood and extended his hand. "Carson Stewart—but please, just Carson. Mr. Stewart sounds much too grown up," he said, while trying to avoid staring deeply into those baby blues. He noted the name on her coffee cup. "Sara is it? You are obviously a drip-coffee-with-one-Splenda girl," Carson said, careful not to blink at the jolt of electricity that traveled up his arm. Slightly stunned at the revelation, Sara replied, "Yes, I'm Representative Becker's communications director, and how did you know what I drink?"

"I'm a damn good journalist," Carson said in a slow, deliberate tone, realizing he was still holding Sara's hand. Sara looked down. Doing her best to maintain a professional attitude, she slowly removed her hand from the extended handshake.

There was something vulnerable about Carson that she wasn't expecting—something in his glance when they first locked eyes. "Well, Ms. Sara Davis, what can I do for you?" he drawled, in an exaggerated Texas accent. As Sara looked up, she thought she must have been mistaken, offended by the sarcastic tone of the journalist she had been expecting.

"I wanted to introduce myself before the interviews. We will be on a very strict schedule tonight," Sara said in a very calm professional manner, careful to downplay her natural southern drawl.

"As you say down here in Texas, this is not my first rodeo, darling. I will be quick and to the point with the congress-woman," Carson replied, smiling at her linguistic attempts. Inside, Sara's inner monologue was waging a full-throttle, verbal rebuttal to this smug excuse of a journalist. Maintaining her composure was only possible by firmly reminding herself of the words her boss said to her earlier, "*Even Carson Stewart deserves a second chance.*"

"I am happy to hear you are prepared and ready to go. We will be meeting in Mrs. Becker's suite for a quick meet-and-greet before heading over to the Ball. You are welcome to join us if you would like," Sara offered in the most matter-of-fact tone she could muster. "The formal interviews will happen at the Ball prior to the doors opening. There will be an interview area set up by the step-and-repeat, near the front door."

Carson found himself distracted again by Sara's beauty, but quickly regained his irritating demeanor. "Will there be food?" he asked, raising his eyebrows in amusement. "I'd be up for an eat-and-repeat while I wait." With every word that exited Carson's mouth, it became increasingly more obvious to Sara why Carson was so despised amongst his peers. She tried her very best to not be judgmental; however, she couldn't help getting in a small jab of her own.

"Yes, there will be food. Just light snacks and no drinks, since it looks like you are already well-watered, as we say here in Texas," Sara drawled, secretly wishing he would skip the meet-and-greet altogether.

Letting go of the light jab, Carson replied, "Great, I will be there. What is the room number?" He grabbed his journal to write down the information.

"There is no number. It's the Presidential Suite on the top floor," Sara responded. "Don't think you'll need to write that down, as you can't miss the only room at the top." She could barely keep from launching her coffee at him.

"A bit presumptuous, wouldn't you say?" Carson added, deliberately scrawling the word "Presidential" in his journal.

Seeing his writing, Sara smiled sweetly and replied, "If you can't find it, we will understand." She turned and walked away, the warmth in her cheeks matching the heat of the fireplace.

Carson sat down, speechless as he watched Sara walk towards the elevators in the hotel lobby. Something inside him, old muscle memory of sorts, had taken over the last several minutes of conversation and saved him from identifying what he was feeling. But deep inside, he felt a stirring that was foreign to him. Something was different about her and he couldn't put his finger on it. For a brief moment, he had the urge to run after her and apologize, asking if they could start over. Silently, Carson was wishing she would stop and look back to give some indication he hadn't completely blown it.

Walking to the elevator, Sara took a long sip of her coffee. Looking down, she noticed the barista had written on the side of her cup in black ink. Bold letters recorded her name and the words, "drip 1 spld." Stepping into the elevator she tapped the button for the top floor. As the doors closed, she was facing a floor to ceiling reflection of herself, which revealed a very flushed face and a slow, creeping smile of amusement.

Carson draped the lanyard attached to the *Common-Perspective.com* press credential around his neck as he approached the doors to the event. Two men from the security team caused Carson to break his stride, as they stopped him to review his press pass. Sara briefly considered requesting that Carson be turned away at the door. However, given his somewhat docile presence at the meet-and-greet, she left his name on the approved press list.

Upon entering through the massive doors to the Ball, Carson navigated a steady stream of volunteers busy with last minute details. A young man, dressed in all black with a headset and clipboard, approached Carson and asked for his name. "Carson Stewart," he replied.

"Perfect, you are up in five minutes. Follow me," the young man beckoned. "Will you be videoing or recording your interview?" he asked while they walked.

"Just recording. I brought my own equipment." Carson was referring to a plug-in microphone he attached to the end of his iPhone, a standard journalistic tool.

Walking up to the backdrop, Carson caught a glimpse of a former colleague finishing up his interview with Clara. Carson's throat constricted as he gripped his journal even tighter. Part of Carson's brain was trying to convince himself he needed a drink. Scanning the room, he quickly located the bar and was mentally making plans to grab a quick shot of Jack

Daniels before his interview. It had been over a week since his last drink, and the fog that had accumulated in his mind for years was beginning to clear. As he was assessing the best detour to the bar, the young man in black grabbed his right arm. Guiding him towards the interview chairs, he pushed back his headset and said, "You are on the clock."

Settling into the comfortable cow print chair, Carson opened his journal to the page he marked. "Great to see you again so soon, Carson," Clara began leaning forward in her chair to shake Carson's hand. Caught off guard, Carson placed his journal in his lap and leaned forward. Shaking hands with the congresswoman, he returned the greeting.

"Congresswoman Becker, thank you for the time tonight," he said sincerely, in a rare moment of gratitude.

"We are excited to have you here on such an exhilarating night. Now what can I answer for you?" Clara asked.

Something was off. After the brief introduction in the suite earlier, and now a warmer introduction at the Ball, Clara Becker was different than the rest. Something just wasn't right and Carson was struggling in the moment to connect the dots. Like the strobe of a neon sign, his strained mind flashed, "NO JUDGMENT." Carson glanced down at his journal and noticed the sweat forming in the palm of his hands. As he quickly read the questions he had prepared, he realized that, thanks to Carson Stewart, Clara Becker's evening was going to be anything but exhilarating.

The battle in his mind raged hotter than Joe's depiction of *Dante's Inferno*. One side desperately pushed Carson to change his line of questioning to "no judgment." The other side convincingly stated the case to stay within his life rules,

"She can't be trusted." Lifting his head to engage his line of questions brought him into full view of Sara Davis, who was standing to the right of the congresswoman. Carson's lip trembled at the sight of Sara. "Sara, can you get Mr. Stewart some water?" Clara asked, noting Carson's unease. Leaning forward, Clara softly inquired, "Are you okay, Mr. Stewart?" Carson felt a rush of blood moving into his head and knew he was becoming lightheaded like a rookie reporter. With a flicker, his reflexes engaged his muscle memory, and years of conditioning took over.

"I am doing a series of articles on your long-term popularity in Congress. It is my belief that there is more to the story than meets the eye," Carson began.

"Is there a question in there, young man?" Clara interjected, as she sat back in her chair.

"My sources tell me yours is a story of power, built upon your well-honed prowess at leaking confidential documents and military secrets. How would you respond to those queries?" Carson challenged, stoic and emotionless.

Clara sat silently, carefully considering her response, as Sara returned with a bottle of water. Clara once again leaned forward in her chair, this time with a facial expression, trained by years of confrontation with some of the toughest people on the planet. Her calm, measured, matter-of-fact tone was an immediate signal to Sara that something had gone extremely wrong. "Mr. Carson, I need you to pay very close attention to what I am about to say," Clara's eyes locked Carson's with the intensity of a laser. "I have never betrayed my country!"

Before Clara could continue Sara stepped into the middle and proclaimed, "We are done here." Placing the bottle of water directly in Carson's face she continued, "And by *we* I mean *you*." She motioned to the security detail hovering in the shadows. Before Carson knew what was happening, two large men had lifted him from his seat and began to forcefully move him toward the exit.

As Carson was being removed, Sara continued, "Mr. Stewart, you were invited tonight as a courtesy. Your line of questions is not only inappropriate but extremely misguided." Carson forcefully shook off the grip of his two escorts.

"I can find the door myself. Been thrown out of better places than this," he said, as he straightened his shirt and jacket. Just before he opened the door, Clara firmly spoke the last word.

"Mr. Stewart, anytime you would like to hear the real story of how I have managed to avoid the situational integrity that plagues the inside of the Beltway, let me know. Until then, we are done." Without looking back, Carson pulled the metal doors open and exited the room.

"I am so sorry, Clara," Sara said with a look of complete mortification.

"Nothing for you to be sorry about, sweetie," Clara said in a gentle tone. "You should know there is always more to be learned behind every question. What we need to discover is what motivated him to ask such a ridiculous question in the first place," Clara continued. "I can't imagine a journalist in his position would jeopardize his comeback and just make something up again."

"What do you want me to do?" Sara asked, face still flushed with frustration.

"Reach out to Kyle Ellis first thing in the morning. Brief him on what just happened. He will know what to do," Clara said. "Now, your immediate orders are to enjoy the evening. Park the past few moments with Mr. Stewart to one side and focus on what is in front of you," Clara continued. Sara's faint smile acknowledged that she realized her mentor was offering another nugget of wisdom.

Leaning in, Sara gently kissed Clara on the cheek and whispered, "Thank you," as she turned to head into the Ball. The doors had opened moments earlier, and a flood of revelers had begun streaming into the main event area. Within a few steps, Sara was swept into a sea of friends, all excited to hear the latest stories of her fast-paced life in D.C. Clara smiled as she watched Sara disappear into the middle of what Clara knew would be a lasting memory for Sara. She also knew, after years in politics, that someone had other plans and was sending her a veiled message. The key was finding out who was behind Carson's inflammatory query before anybody got hurt.

The
DISCOVERY

Kyle Ellis and his team were in full motion after the call from
Sara. The relationship between Clara and Kyle dated back to
college, and his protective instinct had only grown stronger
when she embarked on a career in politics. As the CEO of Ellis International, Kyle was marshaling all his resources behind
exposing the source of Carson's rumors.

Carson Stewart was no stranger to Kyle. On more than
one occasion, Kyle had to unleash a full damage control counterattack after an article of Carson's was published. Kyle's vast
network of information brokers was unmatched. It would
only be a matter of time before he learned the real story.

Kyle Ellis's unique talent had always been the art of understanding people. His ability to cut to the core of an individual and discern their true purpose had given him the
reputation of running the most sought-after PR firm in the
world. Sizing up Carson Stewart was not difficult. Carson was
a textbook case of narcissism, whose one and only motivation
was himself.

The first priority was discovering what was in it for Carson. Given the recent events unfolding in Carson's career, it was safe to deduce Carson wanted back in the game. The radioactive nature of Carson's reputation would mean only someone close to Carson would risk giving him a second chance. Fortunately, the list of friends close to Carson Stewart was short.

It took only two calls for Kyle to track down Carson's new employer, Brian Palmer, at *CommonPerspective.com*. Brian's reputation as a top-notch, respectable journalist in a digital world filled with marginal media hacks was uncontested. The variable in the story was his recent business contract with a rock-bottom journalist who seemed to be going rogue.

Kyle's team was able to put together Carson's itinerary since he signed on with *CommonPerspective.com*. The trip to D.C. was not unusual; yet the fact that Carson found someone to speak to him was somewhat surprising. His reputation preceded him, and Carson's presence in D.C. did not go unnoticed by the media establishment. A source who knew the general manager at the Willard Hotel connected Carson to Ross Horner. From there, the trail led to Congressman Ryan Burr. It was this revelation that immediately caught Kyle's attention, causing a moment of discomfort as he processed what this implied.

Ryan Burr and Kyle Ellis had known each other for years. It was Kyle who first turned down the opportunity to work with Ryan early in his career. As a rising star and a top litigator in New York, Ryan had plans to conquer the world. The secret reputation of Kyle Ellis was exposed to Ryan while he was defending a top CEO on Wall Street. It was through this case that Ryan learned of the man simply known in an elite circle as, "The Kingmaker."

Kyle's reputation to propel an individual to the highest places of power in the world was unmatched. Ryan, hungry for status, would do whatever it took to have Kyle, The Kingmaker, represent him on his quest for the top. Their first meeting would be their last.

After years of dealing with people seeking power and notoriety, Kyle had developed a sixth sense about the void of purpose in someone's life. If a person's purpose in life did not align with the power they sought, Kyle was quick to pass on creating a long-term relationship. Within the initial hour of their first encounter, Kyle knew Ryan had only one ambition—power for purposes of self, not others. This self-motivated drive is the most destructive force on the planet, and it was clear Ryan Burr was destined for professional carnage. It was at that moment that Kyle politely passed on the offer to work with Ryan and walked away.

Kyle had built his reputation and his circle of Kings, as they were called, on the simple premise of centering one's purpose on others. His Kings were among the most powerful people in the world, using their influence to better the lives of those around them. The unintended consequence of Kyle's success was the emergence of a cottage market of competitors who embraced the ideas of self-focus and promised powerful results to Kyle's cast-offs. One such person was Malcolm Claire.

If Kyle's purpose in life was to perpetuate a chain of helping others, then Malcolm's purpose was simple—to perpetuate a chain of helping others to help him. The line of potential, self-seeking clients was never ending. With offices in New York City and D.C., Malcolm's powerbase was well established. Anyone looking for a ride to the top on the backs of others, needed to look no further than Malcolm Claire.

Kyle sat motionless for a few moments as he processed his findings. The name of Ryan Burr in connection with Carson Stewart meant only one thing; Malcolm Claire's fingerprints were all over this. Breaking his trance, he glanced at his phone and tapped out a quick message to Clara.

Kyle: *"Ryan Burr connected to Carson Stewart."*

Clara: *"Knew something was up. When can you talk?"*

Kyle: *"Mac and I will be in Dallas tomorrow."*

Clara: *"Perfect. See you then."*

The discovery of a Ryan Burr connection could only lead to one conclusion: Clara was in the crosshairs of something potentially disastrous. Kyle just needed a few more hours to track down the truth behind the story brewing in Carson Stewart's mind.

The private jet touched down effortlessly on Runway 13 Left at Love Field in Dallas, Texas. As Kyle guided the gulfstream onto the taxiway, Mac texted the car service to ensure their vehicle was ready. A native of Texas, Kyle enjoyed visiting Dallas at every opportunity. Mac, who served as Kyle's driver, security detail, and close friend, was raised on the East Coast and found Texas a bit too over-the-top for his taste.

"Car is ready boss!" Mac called out over the Bose headsets.

"Looks like we will be a few minutes early to our meeting for a change," Kyle replied with a hint of amusement in his voice. "Perfect day in Dallas; cold but sunny," he continued, assessing the weather conditions.

"Considering it was snowing when we left the City, it's a low bar for perfect," Mac replied with a smile.

Once in the driver's seat of the black suburban, Mac merged onto Lemmon Ave and headed south towards downtown. The drive to the central business district was just a few minutes from the inner-city airport. Navigating through Dallas construction zones was like dusting for the fingerprints of Clara Becker. The cranes, detours, and hard hats dotting the major thoroughfares gave ample testimony about her economic impact on the booming North Texas economy. Despite the powerful economic initiatives that were thriving, the drive through town was also a constant reminder of the work still needed. Even in a city prospering like Dallas, medians collected impoverished people holding cardboard signs telling their story. Clara would be the first to agree that there was still much work to be done.

Mac always insisted Kyle ride in the backseat as he drove, mostly for safety purposes. Kyle scanned his phone for the latest update from the office. "Looks like we have what we were looking for, Mac," Kyle proclaimed.

"Any surprises?" Mac asked, glancing in the rearview mirror.

"Unfortunately, no," Kyle said in a deflated tone. "The length Malcolm will go to get what he wants has never surprised me." Kyle continued to scan his phone for clues.

As Kyle glanced up from his phone, he looked out the side window of the suburban, noting the dichotomy between the construction cranes and the homeless signs. "Reminds me of the City," Kyle said almost under his breath. "Let's stop before we leave and grab some water and snacks to hand out when we depart," Kyle continued, never taking his eyes off the scene at the corner.

"Absolutely, boss. I can make a run while you are having lunch with the congresswoman," Mac nodded.

"Thanks, Mac."

Clara Becker met her husband, Luis Santiago, in college. They married after graduation, squeezing in a wedding during Clara's first run for public office. She was elected mayor of the small central Texas town where she was raised. To avoid confusion after the campaign, Luis urged Clara to keep her maiden name while in public office. Little did they know, almost 25 years later, she would still be holding public office.

A successful businessman, Luis had offices around the country, with headquarters in Austin. The Dallas office was growing at a pace that required Luis to keep a small apartment nearby. For Clara, the Dallas apartment became a welcome getaway from the fast-paced life of politics and the sterile hotel environment. The uptown area high-rise offered views of downtown Dallas that rivaled any city skyline in the country, especially at night.

Centrally located, Clara arranged to meet Kyle for lunch at a spot within walking distance of her place. Stepping onto

McKinney Ave, Clara turned left and walked a few short blocks. At the first light, she tapped a quick note to Sara.

Clara: *"Having lunch with Kyle. Meet us at Klyde Warren after lunch."*

Sara: *"Will do. Text me when you are heading that way."*

Looking up, Clara realized the light had turned green and she hustled across the busy street. Another block and she turned left once again, and traveled two short blocks to her destination. Tucked into the shadows of the towering Dallas Federal Reserve Bank was the nondescript *Sammy's Bar-B-Q*, a Dallas restaurant landmark. The history of this legendary establishment was displayed on the walls as well as recorded on the plates.

Mac pulled the black suburban into *Sammy's* side lot. "Text me when you are ready. I am on my way to grab supplies for later," Mac said as he positioned the suburban in the lot.

"Thanks Mac. Might be here a few hours. Grab some lunch while you are out," Kyle said as he slid out of the back-seat.

The smell of smoked brisket filled the cool, crisp air as Kyle walked up to the aging, black metal front door. The old building had survived the crush of new construction surrounding it on all sides. The green, painted brick facade told a story of years past, providing a faded glimpse of the original 1930s grocery store that previously inhabited the place. Once inside, Kyle was greeted by fifty-year-old tables and chairs, arranged across the bare concrete floor. There is a strategy to eating at *Sammy's*. The key is arriving early because once the barbeque is gone, they are done serving meat for the day.

However, for many latecomers, the one caveat is that the side dishes and veggies often rival the smoked meat. The farm-fresh ingredients, coupled with family recipes passed down through generations, make the culinary accouterments memorable for everyone.

Kyle was greeted almost immediately by the familiar voice of Clara Becker. "Hey there, sweetheart," Clara announced across the cavernous room. The line to order had already wrapped around the interior of the building. Even a congresswoman had to wait her turn with the Pit Master. Kyle walked up to Clara and wrapped his arms around his dearest friend.

"Emily sends her best and wants you to know how much she misses you," Kyle said, knowing how much his wife wished she could have joined the lunch.

Clara looked at Kyle with deep affection. "I miss that girl tremendously. Please send my love. Your friendship is only matched by her."

As they made their way into line, Kyle couldn't help but notice the clientele in the bustling restaurant. It was a smorgasbord of suits and jeans, a true crossroads of life in the city. Standing amidst the hungry masses, Kyle was again awed by the congresswoman who was willing to wait patiently in line. The humility and integrity of Clara Becker was unrivaled, which made his recent discovery all the more difficult to share. Working to keep the conversation light until they were able to order and retreat to their seats, Kyle pressed Clara for her favorite item on the menu.

"Brisket sandwich with potato casserole—hands down the best in the state," declared Clara without missing a beat.

The person directly in front of Clara, in perfect Texas fashion, turned to heartily agree with the congresswoman.

"Then it's settled," Kyle replied, as he stepped up to place their order with the Pit Master. "Two brisket sandwiches please," said Kyle.

"Sliced or chopped?" came the reply. A quick glance at Clara finished the order.

"Sliced for me," she nodded.

"Two sliced, please."

The two slid their green trays down the line to review the side options and gather their final order. The main dining room had filled to capacity, forcing them to find a table on the outside deck. The remote seating was serendipitous for Kyle, given the conversation that needed to happen.

Once settled, Clara wasted no time with her question, "What have you found out?"

Kyle, without hesitation, responded, "It seems Malcolm Claire is working with Burr."

Clara stopped mid bite to look up at Kyle, "That can never be good," she said, chewing thoughtfully.

"We have discovered it is worse than no good," Kyle said. "It seems Ryan has an unhealthy fixation on becoming president. My sources tell me his people are cooking up something to propel him into the spotlight, just in time for the primary season to ramp up into full gear."

Clara placed her brisket sandwich back on the plate. "If Malcolm Claire is involved, someone is going to get hurt," she announced, "and I mean that both figuratively and literally."

"I am afraid you are his target," Kyle said in a soft whisper, the gravity of the discussion settling over the table.

"Can't say I am surprised. Ryan has been bitter ever since I gave him the ultimatum to clean up his act or face my allegations of ethics violations," Clara confessed.

"How does Carson play into this?" she asked. "I know he has written controversial articles in the past, but this seems a little beyond his scope."

"From what I have learned, Carson is the trigger. His article, which was intended to be a piece about your long-standing integrity in D.C., is being high-jacked," Kyle said. "Seems the combination of Carson's ego-driven desire to get back into the game, coupled with his downward spiral into a bottle, was the perfect storm for Malcolm. The only guidance I do not yet have is the timing. Our team is ahead of this, however, and we have a plan in place for a couple of different scenarios that could play out," Kyle assured Clara.

Clara picked up her sandwich and with a look of temporary relief, began to eat her lunch. "Kyle, old friend, you have always been there for me. Thank you. I have no doubt this will be no different. Let's enjoy our lunch," Clara offered as she wiped sauce from her chin.

The
BETRAYAL

Clara texted Sara as she walked with Kyle a few blocks to the park. "The walk will do me good after all that barbeque," Clara said, never looking up from her phone. As the light turned green, the two crossed the street to enter the east edge of the park. Stepping onto the crushed granite pathway, they strolled under the arches of a tree-lined trail leading to the central pavilion.

"There is Sara," Clara smiled as she raised her hand to acknowledge her vibrant, young staff member.

"She has been a tremendous addition to your team," Kyle added, as he spotted her in the distance. "She reminds me of the younger you," he commented cheerfully, pleased that Clara had found such loyal assistance.

"She certainly does," Clara confirmed.

Sara's infectious smile could brighten any conversation. Her naturally optimistic view on life had not been tarnished, even after years inside the Beltway. "Kyle, it is great to see you! Welcome to Dallas," came the typical, energetic greeting from Sara. Kyle skipped Sara's extended hand, and gave her a hug.

"Thank you for ordering the perfect weather for my trip," Kyle said with a wink.

"Looks like we are going to have our hands full with Carson," Clara stated. "Kyle and I have spent some time this afternoon discussing our options."

"What can I do to help?" Sara offered, looking at both Clara and Kyle for guidance. "That is a great question, Sara. It is our belief Carson is being used by Ryan Burr—we just don't know to what end," Kyle said.

"Sara, we need to know what the end game is so we can have a plan in place to handle anything they throw at us," Clara added. "I need to ask you to do something," Clara paused, thoughtfully.

"Name it," Sara said without hesitation. She had seen that look on Clara's face before, and knew this situation called for action—and quickly.

Casually strolling through the park, Kyle and Clara outlined a strategy for Sara to connect with Carson, in order to gain insight into his plan. "We don't know what we are up against, but we do know that with Malcolm Claire involved, it could get ugly fast," Kyle noted. "Our first concern, of course, is for your safety," he added as Clara shook her head in agreement. "At the first sign of trouble, we want you out. Mac will have some of his friends watching over you from a distance, but you still need to be very aware of the situation," he said with a stern, father-like tone. "Ryan Burr and Malcolm Claire cannot be trusted, so therefore, neither can Carson Stewart."

Reaching the end of the park, they came to a street where there were two black suburbans waiting. Before climbing in the backseat, Kyle looked at Sara one more time. "You will be getting some additional details from my office later today. Be ready to leave for New York by tomorrow." With one last hug, he climbed in the back seat and closed the door. Clara slipped her arm under Sara's elbow as they watched Kyle and Mac pull away.

"Come dear, let me give you a ride back home," Clara said in a soft voice. The two climbed into the waiting SUV for the short drive to Sara's family home in Highland Park.

"I can't tell you how much I appreciate what you are doing for me," Clara said, shifting restlessly in the backseat.

"Nothing you wouldn't do for me," Sara replied without hesitation.

"Sweetie, you should know I am a big believer in guardian angels. I will reach out with a special request for you," Clara said with a motherly smile. Sara reached over and squeezed Clara's hand, meeting her gaze with a smile of her own.

The
CITY

Carson read and reread the text message multiple times as he finished getting ready. The same thought kept running through his mind, "Why would Sara Davis want to meet for dinner?" His conflicted emotions were overwhelming: On one hand, Sara's close connection to Clara Becker could provide key insights for his article. Yet, for the first time in years, Carson Stewart actually felt something for a woman. It must be serious, he thought to himself as he stood looking at the reflection in the small mirror. The feelings he was experiencing were as foreign to him as the tie hanging around his neck. After a few moments, Carson blinked. "Okay, snap out of it. This is just business. Get your head in the game," he said out loud in a tone of voice intended to be convincing.

Sara perched on the edge of the bathtub in a robe and wrapped her damp hair in a towel. She couldn't help but notice the palms of her hands sweating as her mind repeated the mantra that tonight was all business—not a date. Yet, she could feel her body tremble ever so slightly. Neatly displayed on the bed were three options for tonight. The dark, yet

modern business suit that screamed D.C. lawyer was quickly
eliminated. That left two choices. The first, tight leather pants
paired with an angora sweater and striped scarf, represented
the polar opposite of the D.C. business suit. "Too extreme,"
she thought. "Tonight calls for middle-of-the-road." She
reached for her dark skinny jeans and a knee-length, camel
hair, single-breasted coat that she had found at her favorite
vintage boutique. She added the Christian Louboutin red
suede pumps that Clara had given her last Christmas, with a
demand to lighten up and have some fun. "Well, this may not
be fun or light, but these could double as a weapon if needed,"
she smirked. With her outfit settled, Sara began to prepare for
an interview of her own. She hoped her line of questioning
would reveal what Carson Stewart was planning. "How bad
could it be? It's just dinner," she kept reminding herself, while
wiping her sweaty palms on the camel hair.

Carson walked briskly to *Mercer Kitchen*. Located in the
historic Mercer Hotel in SoHo, the two-level restaurant was a
hidden bohemian gem amongst eateries in the City. Entering
the hotel on Prince Street brought Carson directly into the
hotel bar. Quickly scanning the intimate space, Carson immediately located Sara waiting in front of the expansive bookcase
in the hotel lobby. The burgeoning crowd separating them
afforded Carson a brief moment to observe Sara before she
spotted him across the room. Rarely, if ever, did Carson give
women a second look. Tonight, Sara's natural beauty stopped
Carson cold in his tracks and he wished he had arrived earlier
to calm his nerves at the bar. After only a few seconds, Sara
glanced Carson's way and their eyes met. They exchanged a

polite wave, and the two walked toward each other, meeting in the hotel lobby.

"Good evening." Sara smiled, tucking her sweaty hands back into her coat. Carson smiled nervously, as her blue eyes pierced through him once again.

"Good evening to you too," he managed while diverting his eyes to the eclectic surroundings.

"What a beautiful place; I had no idea this was here," Sara continued, surveying the funky decor.

"Yes, it's one of the treasures in SoHo. It used to be an artist's loft years ago until they repurposed it into a hotel and restaurant," Carson snapped back into his investigative journalist persona. "The real treat is downstairs, so I hope you're hungry," Carson pointed the way towards the stairs.

"I wish I could think of a more ladylike way to say this, but I am *starving*," Sara emphasized with a grin.

"Then you have come to the right place," Carson said, guiding her elbow towards the smell of tantalizing cuisine. "Let's head downstairs. We're just in time for our reservation."

As they emerged into the heart of the *Mercer Kitchen*, Sara scanned the cavernous space. "Oh my goodness, this is truly amazing," she exclaimed, forgetting her mission for a moment. The historic basement was really a series of spaces separated by thick brick archways. This allowed patrons a view of the entire space, yet it did not compromise an intimate evening. The open kitchen concept provided a front row seat to all the action in this highly acclaimed restaurant. Carson immediately confirmed their reservation, and they were escorted to their seats. Their table allowed for an unobstructed view of the hectic kitchen, providing them with the perfect setting for their evening.

On cue, a young, statuesque lady approached their table with a wine list and some water. "Will you be starting the evening with something to drink?" she began, setting down the water in front of them. Carson paused and looked at Sara, hoping she would give some indication as to what she was going to order.

"Nothing for me. I am good with water," Sara said, glancing over the menu. "Sparkling or still?" the young lady asked politely.

"Sparkling, please," Sara replied, glancing at Carson as she scanned the dinner options.

Carson disregarded the wine menu, simply saying, "I will have what she is having."

This drew a not-so-discreet glance from Sara, who set her menu down in surprise. "Don't be so shocked. I have been making some changes of late," Carson said candidly.

"I can appreciate that," Sara replied, with approval.

"Wish I could say it has been an easy choice but it hasn't. It is a choice I need to make," he continued.

"Why is that?" Sara asked.

"I've been reflecting on the past several years and what has become very obvious is that I tend to make poor choices after I have been drinking," Carson said, in a rare moment of transparency. Catching his vulnerability, he hurried to lighten the conversation, "And besides, I didn't want to make any bad choices tonight," he continued, playfully paying her an off-handed compliment. Sara felt her heart skip a single beat, and she stumbled to regain composure. For Carson, this was the first true compliment he had offered to a woman in over five years. Something inside him was shifting and embarking on new territory. Carson was the person who could fill a bookshelf with stories about using women to meet his needs, only to discard them the moment he became vulnerable. Tonight, in the basement of the historic hotel, Carson Stewart began a new chapter in his story.

Throughout the evening, the conversation went back and forth between politics, work, and just life. Time stood still for both Carson and Sara, as they lost themselves in good food and better conversation. There was a softening in Carson's gaze that assured Sara that she had slowly earned his trust. At one point in the evening, Sara excused herself for a quick break to the ladies' room. The brief walk, which led back beneath the stairs, allowed Sara just enough time to process the evening. Pushing open the rounded door, it became evident in her mind that her assessment of Carson Stewart was changing. She felt confident in his altruistic intentions to write a true story about Clara. More importantly, Sara was observing a side of Carson that few, if any, knew existed.

Carson and Sara exited the hotel, and walked along Prince Avenue to 6th as the boulevards began to fill with people. The energy at this time of night was more laid back than Midtown, with a true artistic vibe. Suddenly spontaneous, Carson asked, "Do you by any chance like macaroons?" Sara couldn't decide which was more shocking—the fact Carson just picked the one treat Sara was crazy about, or the fact that Carson had ever heard of a macaroon. She smiled and took the bait.

"I love macaroons," she said, wondering why she still had an appetite after cleaning her plate at dinner.

"Excellent! Turn here on Broadway and I will treat you to what some claim to be the best macaroons in the City," he said with a wry smile of satisfaction and relief.

Nibbling the delightful treat from *Laduree*, the macaroon capital of New York City, the two strolled along, their constant conversation fueled by common curiosity and the amazingly delicate macaroon. After a few short blocks, Carson realized he had inadvertently wandered towards *Joe's Place*. Approaching the nondescript entrance Carson gently inquired, "If you have a few more minutes, there's someone I'd like you to meet. I know it's not much to look at, but this is his establishment." Sara smiled and eyed the battered door.

"And where are we?" she asked, happy to extend the evening for a while.

"You might call this my home away from home," Carson said.

"Are you sure it's safe to go in there?" Sara asked, studying the neighborhood and the nondescript location.

Carson chuckled and replied, "Safer in there than in any legislative session you'll be going back to." Gently placing his hand on the small of her back, he softly guided her down the stairs and through the well-worn door.

Once inside, Sara noticed a small crowd of old-timers gathered around the bar, transfixed by the storyteller serving them drinks. Carson caught Joe's eye as he was mid-sentence, flawlessly pouring drinks and telling yarns that kept the atmosphere lively. Not spotting Sara immediately, Joe held up a single glass without missing a beat—a private code signaling whether Carson wanted his usual.

Sliding in between a couple patrons, Carson made room for Sara and she was able to slide onto a stool into Joe's view. Shaking off Joe's drink offer, Carson motioned to Sara, "Joe, I want you to meet Sara. Sara, this is Joe, my bartender and resident philosopher." Carson spoke as though having a personal bartender was a normal relationship.

"Nice to meet you, Joe," Sara's elevated voice competed with the noisy crowd. As Joe made eye contact while reaching to shake her outstretched hand, he stood frozen for a moment, unable to hide his disbelief. Eyes darting from Carson to Sara, Joe forgot to let go of her hand until she looked at Carson in confusion.

"Don't look so surprised, Joe. I've been out with a lady before," Carson said, as he reached over to awkwardly break Joe's grip on Sara.

Joe remained unusually stoic, unable to speak until he finally blinked. "Yes, but not with someone as intelligent and beautiful as Ms. Sara, here. It is nice to meet you, Sara," Joe said, turning quickly to avoid eye contact. Carson could have sworn he saw Joe's eyes soften, and a small tear gathering at the corner. He knew Joe had often worried about his ability to relate with women, but he'd never seen him like this.

Within a moment, Joe was his old self, turning with a flourish. "What will you have, the usual?" Joe asked as he was pulling up clean glasses from behind the bar.

"Mineral water for me tonight, Joe. I am walking this young lady home," Carson said. Joe was clearly smiling behind his full beard.

"Nice choice. It just so happens we are well known in the City for our mineral water. And for you, Ms. Sara—what will you have?" asked Joe with a tender smile.

Before she could answer, Carson spoke up, "Black coffee with one splenda for the lady," he said with a smile. Sara paused to absorb the fullness of the compliment just paid her. She could feel her cheeks begin to blush as a wash of warmth blanketed her body.

"Well since you are so famous for your mineral water, maybe I should give that a try tonight," Sara said smiling, while leaning on the bar with her head tilted to look Carson in the eyes.

"Probably best given the hour. You can trust that Joe knows what he's talking about when it comes to mineral water," Carson said in a gentle voice, almost inaudible while returning the smile.

Joe slid the lid of the cooler open to produce two cold bottles of *Topo Chico*. With a single flip of the wrist, he popped the top off both bottles and poured the contents into frosted glasses. "The frosted glasses make all the difference," Joe said as he placed the glasses on drink coasters.

Taking the first drink, Sara quickly agreed, "Yes, that is the best mineral water I have ever had."

Carson actually snickered out loud, "Joe has always said that the best way to trust someone is to trust him." Sara choked on her drink and looked at Joe.

"That's a quote from Hemingway, isn't it?" Sara inquired, trying to see beyond the beard. She recognized the quote immediately. Her dad used to tell her the same thing when he would throw her up in the air as a child. Her love of literature was instilled by her father, who was always quick with a quote, poem, or word of wisdom from his journalistic memory. Sara knew there was more going on in Joe's brain than the next drink order. Joe startled, and grabbed her bottle.

"I think it's Hemingway. Can't quite remember," Joe said, pouring the last bit into Sara's glass. "On the house," he declared as he tossed the bottle into the recycle bin.

Carson watched with amusement, "You must have made quite the impression. I haven't seen Joe give away a drink in years," Carson said, as he raised his glass to gently tap Sara's full drink. Joe quietly slipped into the back room while the two settled in.

Carson and Sara sat at the end of Joe's bar for another hour, absorbed in laughter and funny stories they recounted from their youth. Never far away, Joe kept his eye on them both, his mind clearly racing as he watched the flushed face of Sara capture Carson's full attention

Carson insisted on walking Sara back to her hotel. They waved a quick goodbye to Joe, and continued their conversation the entire walk. Before they knew it, they were both standing in front of their destination, engulfed by the first awkward silence of the night. The moment quickly passed as Carson presented his hand for a goodnight handshake. With a relieved smile, Sara leaned in and ever-so-gently kissed Carson on the right cheek while whispering softly, "Thank you for a wonderful evening, Mr. Stewart." With that gesture, she quickly turned to step into the lobby of her hotel. Carson stood silently and watched as Sara weaved through the crowd of people and disappeared into the bank of elevators. With an unfamiliar feeling inside, and an unaccustomed grin on his face, he turned and walked home.

The
CHOICE

Upon entering his dark apartment, Carson sensed something was not right. A flip of the switch on the wall cast a dim, yellowish glow over the room. Scanning the room quickly revealed nothing, until his eyes focused on the small table next to his favorite chair. A large manila envelope had been left in plain view.

Carson's heart began to race slightly as he retraced his steps before he left his apartment earlier. He clearly remembered sitting in his chair to tie his shoes before walking out the door. Nothing in his memory included a large manila envelope. Without realizing what he was doing, Carson had been backing away from the table and quickly came into contact with the wall. The sudden collision caused him to startle and let out a burst of nervous energy by dropping to his knees.

Once he realized what happened, he stood up and headed over to examine the envelope. Making a point to turn on every light in the small apartment, Carson casually checked any potential hiding spots, resisting the urge to look under the bed like he used to do as a child. Gently sitting on the edge of the chair, he carefully picked up the envelope to examine its contents. Inside were several documents stamped TOP SECRET in red ink across the top. Each page contained several thick black lines of redacted text. Scanning each page quickly, Carson soon realized that he was holding correspondence between the NSA and members of the House Intelligence Committee.

Carson knew he was in possession of what many in the media would consider the Holy Grail: top-secret documents. Scanning each page, he began quickly piecing together the narrative between the heavily redacted texts. Towards the bottom of the first page, he came across a name that caused him to pause: Congresswoman Clara Becker. Carson's mind began to race as he considered this revelation. The ethical conflict brewing in his thoughts was more overwhelming than the urge to silence it with a drink. The last several hours with Sara had convinced him Congresswoman Clara Becker was not only who everyone said she was, but also more. Now, he held government documents contradicting every word Sara said, and rewriting a story of betrayal and possible treason.

On the short walk from Sara's hotel to his apartment, Carson had all but written his first installment on Clara Becker in his mind. Sara had effectively laid the foundation for what would be a series, each installment extolling the many wonderful works of the congresswoman's career. Now, holding what appeared to be the proverbial smoking gun, Carson had to make a choice. He knew deep inside, the sensational nature of these documents would propel him back into the spotlight and erase his stain with the national press.

The quiver in his body sent clear messages to his brain, convincing him that only a drink could calm his nerves and give him clarity. Stuffing the pages back into the envelope, Carson scanned the room for someplace safe to hide the contents. Overcome with anxiety, he tossed the envelope into the freezer compartment of his refrigerator. He had once heard that besides the bank itself, the freezer was the safest spot to stash cash and important documents. Closing the door of the freezer, he leaned his head against the refrigerator, trying to process all that was happening. More than a drink, Carson realized he needed someone to talk to, someone he trusted to help him sort through the difficult choices he needed to make.

Joe's Place had dwindled down to its last customers when Carson stepped into the bar for the second time that evening. Joe was making the final preparations to close when Carson took a seat. The look on Carson's face was all Joe needed to prompt his authoritative bark to the remaining customers, "Time to close up folks; the last drink is on me." For the second time in one day, Carson witnessed Joe giving away free drinks.

Joe turned the lock in the old wooden door as the last two people exited the bar, giving Joe and Carson some time alone. Stepping back behind the bar, Joe pulled a mineral water from the cooler, popped the top, and began to pour the contents into a glass. "Female trouble?" Joe prodded, never looking up from the glass.

"Not exactly," Carson spoke slowly. "In fact, I'm not quite sure I would know where to begin." Carson's head was firmly planted in his hands.

"Why not just tell me what brought you back here tonight," Joe offered, sliding the cold drink across the bar.

"I need to make a professional choice, and I am conflicted on which way to turn," Carson began, clearly tormented by his situation. Not responding, Joe allowed Carson to continue. "My gut tells me one thing, but my eyes are telling me something else."

Joe poured a second glass of water and took a drink. "Which do you think is true?" he asked, prompting Carson to sort it out.

"How can I really know? What I have seen certainly looked true to me," Carson said.

"And your gut, is it not a good measure of truth?" Joe asked, clearly sensing that Carson had seen something conflicting. Carson sat with both hands wrapped around the glass in front of him, contemplating Joe's last question.

Finally speaking, he said, "It sure *feels* true."

"Your choice is secondary to your first priority—find the truth," Joe said. "The young college kid that used to come in here years ago always strained to find the truth, no matter the cost. He wouldn't settle for less or make decisions without it," Carson knew he was referring to him. It was so easy in the early days; find the truth and write about the truth. It was hard to pinpoint the moment in his career when the truth became boring and unprofitable. Gradually, over time, Carson had slipped into the all-consuming trap of feeding the lie of sensational journalism. Trying to construct a reputation more grandiose than the Hearst Castle at San Simeon, Carson knew he was no longer building on a foundation of truth. Truth became more relative than the foundation his reputation was built upon.

"How can I know truth—in fact, how can anyone know truth these days?" Carson inquired.

"That, my friend, is connected to one of the choices of life," Joe replied as he wiped the bar top out of habit.

"Wait a minute, there are life choices that I haven't considered?" Carson asked in a deliberately sarcastic tone.

"I think you know more than you give yourself credit for," Joe retorted, ignoring the sarcasm. "Truth is anchored to a fixed set of morals and principles. Truth does not deceive." Carson processed the words carefully, trying to recall where he had heard this before.

"Where does it say anything about winning?" Carson asked.

"You see, that is the problem with truth; it is often the badge of honor worn by the losers and beggars of this world." Joe could sense the battle between right and wrong waging war inside Carson. The definition of success that had claimed victory over Carson's life for so many years was slowly consuming him.

Pushing his glass to the edge of the bar, Carson stood from his chair. "Think I'm going to need something a bit stronger than mineral water and more watered down than truth, my good friend," Carson said in a deliberate tone.

"Can't help you there, since we're officially closed and my library hasn't been watered down since I removed most of the dailies," Joe replied, locking the cash register.

"Well, that's the beautiful thing about the City—you can always get a drink. Even at 3:00 a.m.," Carson said as he walked toward the door.

"You going to be okay?" Joe asked, as Carson retreated.

Pausing as he placed his hand on the handle of the door, Carson let his head down slightly. Softly, he spoke before walking into the cold dark night, "The choice is clear. I have to watch out for me, because no one else will."

Standing resolute behind the bar, Joe warned, "Turning your back on truth means becoming the face of its murderous offspring—the face of a liar is not one you want to wake up to every day. If others get hurt in the process, there is no honor in your actions or decisions." With those words ringing in his troubled conscience, Carson exited the bar and combed the City to find the affirmation he desired at the bottom of a glass of whiskey.

The
DECEPTION

Carson faced his laptop with a bottle of Jameson Black Barrel Whiskey to one side, and a glass to the other. The only time Carson lifted his fingers from the keyboard was to take another drink and review what he had just written. The letters became words at an astonishing rate, as he wrote the first installment in the series he titled simply, *The Deception*.

The glow of the morning sun began to fill the small room. Time had melted away before Carson lifted his hands and leaned back into the stiff, wooden chair. Staring at the screen with glassy eyes, he lifted the final glass of whiskey slowly to his lips. In one final drink, the remaining contents of the glass disappeared. With deliberate ease, he placed the glass back on the table. Rolling his finger across the track pad on his laptop, he maneuvered the cursor across the screen, tapping his finger as he went. Within moments, the document had been saved and attached to an email to Brian at *The Common Perspective*. With one last tap of the finger, the familiar swoosh sound broke the silence, indicating the article was now in route to its final destination. Carson was back in the game, or so he believed. Little did he know, the true deception had just begun with the simple stroke of a key.

Malcolm Claire pressed send on his phone. Only the person on the other end could understand the code. Placing the phone inside the front breast pocket of his jacket, he looked out the window of his midtown, high-rise office. His view allowed him an unobstructed vista of the City looking north. The clear skies framed a breathtaking scene, and only the vibration in his jacket could break his momentary awe. Removing his phone, he read the return message, *"Continue."*

The flag-lined corridors of the Longworth Office building were always crowded with people. Sara Davis maneuvered her way through the sea of suits, rarely looking up from her phone. The tears forming in her eyes made it more difficult to focus as her fingers tapped out the text message. *"How could you do that?"* she wrote.

Out of instinct, she pulled up from her brisk-paced walk at an entrance marked with a large plaque, which read: "REPRESENTATIVE, Clara Becker, Texas." She wiped her eyes before passing through the deep doorway into the office suite. Her heart racing, Sara took in a deep breath and entered the congresswoman's office.

Clara was known to be in the office early, even for a representative, and today she was there even earlier. Sara quickly and quietly approached Clara's desk. Looking up from her laptop, Clara's face revealed she had seen the online story that broke early that morning. The accusations against the congresswoman were fierce, primarily focusing on the treasonous exposure of key undercover operatives within the world's largest terrorist cell. The information linked recent acts of terror to a trail of leaked information allegedly from the highest-ranking member of Congress, Clara Becker. The article hinted at a follow-up, suggesting Clara Becker's true secret of success was her abuse of power through blackmail and the documented selling of secrets.

Sara spoke first. "I am so sorry, Clara," she said, using the Congresswoman's first name for the first time in years. "When I left him in the City, he assured me the piece he was writing would reveal the truth behind your success. His intention was to focus on your integrity. This was never part of the conversation." Sara found it difficult not to choke up.

Clara Becker had been in politics too long to not read what was happening. Her first concern was for her young staff member, and the obvious wound she had received. Walking around her desk, Clara embraced Sara with the hug of a mother. Sara rested her head on Clara's shoulder and began to sob uncontrollably. The gentle touch of Clara's hand assured Sara that there was a way through this. Sara had heard the same words hundreds of times throughout the years from Clara, "There is always a way through, if you stay true to who you are." For the team surrounding Clara Becker, the next several days would be a genuine test of those words.

Joe's phone vibrated twice, alerting him to an incoming text message. Placing his cup of coffee on the table, he retrieved his phone to read the message from a trusted source. The message revealed a clickable link. Tapping on the link revealed the online story written by Carson Stewart, which clearly indicated that he had made his choice. Joe's furrowed brow darkened as he finished the article. His eyes wandered across the room, settling on the single framed picture resting on a small table in the corner. From another pocket inside his jacket, Joe produced a second phone. Scrolling through the list of codes, he tapped on the name he was looking for. The message was decipherable to only one recipient, *"Washington1300."* For the second time, Joe excused his customers with drinks on the house. Grabbing his coat, he locked the bar and set out for Washington Square Park. Joe was also a man who knew that the day would come to call in a favor. Today was that day.

The
REVELATION

Carson gripped the phone even tighter as he reread the text message from Sara. Numerous times, he began to write a response, only to erase his feeble attempts at an explanation. For a person whose career was built on words, he sadly found himself without anything to say. From the moment he hit send, he knew he had made his choice. The choice closed all roads between his relationship with Sara and the truth about Clara Becker. The mysterious documents painting a deeply disturbing story of corruption had also written him back into the pages of notoriety. Somehow, the old high of making headlines was replaced by the low throb of a headache.

In the mist of recovering from what was proving to be a massive hangover, Carson finally found brief moments of clarity. Rethinking the last several sleepless hours created waves of nausea and regret. He never questioned where the documents came from, nor did he question the validity of the information. Given the sheer amount of redacted lines within the pages, even a rookie journalist would have recognized the red flags. His rush to embrace what he felt was truth now had him second-guessing his actions.

Carson never noticed the black SUV that pulled up across the street from the park bench he had been sitting on since daybreak. Behind darkened windows, the passenger read the text message on his phone. "We are a go," he said quietly, eying Carson through tinted glass. With one fluid motion, a man dressed in a black suit with a black shirt and dark sunglasses exited the back door of the SUV. He carried a leather attaché under his arm as he walked across the street towards Carson. With military precision, the man placed the attaché on the bench within Carson's reach without being detected. As quickly as he appeared he was gone, vanishing into the densely wooded background.

Moments had passed before Carson noticed the dark leather attaché lying next to him. The small envelope tucked under the front flap was addressed to Carson. Instantly jumping from the bench, Carson frantically scanned the park, knowing he was being watched. Carefully, Carson reached down and extracted the handwritten card from inside the envelope. *"You can know what is true,"* was handwritten in blue ink across the white card.

Carson stood motionless, holding the card while staring at the bag. His mind was racing with an endless stream of questions, each creating temporary paralysis. It was the presence of an older lady, pulling her two-wheeled basket, that snapped Carson into the present. "That your bag?" the lady announced, as she claimed one end of the park bench. Carson looked at her, but no words came out of his mouth. Watching as she reached for the bag, Carson lunged forward to retrieve it from the bench. Pulling the bag close to his chest, he turned to leave, hastened by the surprising rash of obscenities uncharacteristic of an old lady.

Finding a safe haven at the Bobst Library on Washington Avenue, Carson crouched at a table amongst a stack of books. Opening the flap, he found an off-white folder outlined in red. The front cover of the folder contained a black box with the words TOP SECRET in larger type. Worn and tattered from handling, the file contained a series of initials and dates along the edges. Unraveling the red cord from the front cover, Carson removed the contents and set them on the table.

In the quiet of the library, Carson read through each document. He quickly realized he was reading the same documents that mysteriously appeared in his apartment. This time, there were no omissions. The copy Carson held was cleared of redacted text, revealing the entire report. Stunned, Carson immediately scanned the room and located the nearest wastebasket, expelling the contents in his stomach. His head spinning, he stumbled backwards until he made contact with the wall. Slowly, he slid down until he came to rest on the floor, still clutching the wastebasket in his arms. The waves of nausea were relentless and the vomiting quickly turned into dry heaves, as there remained nothing left to expel. He knew this was the metaphor for the rest of his life. His words were nothing but the dry heaves of lies. Joe's words rang in his ears as he hung his head, "The face of a liar is not one you want to wake up to every day."

"You okay?" came a soft female voice from across the room. Carson pulled his head up to see a young college student standing motionless in front of him.

"Yes, just don't eat the tacos," Carson said as he made his way back to his feet. "And don't study journalism!" he added with too much intensity.

The young college student was relieved to find Carson alive and responded, "I never eat on campus. And don't worry, I want to study something with integrity," she added as she turned to walk away. Placing the vomit-laden wastebasket on the floor, Carson moved back to the document that exposed his lies. The full story, according to the complete report, painted a much different picture than Carson had presented to the world. Carson realized that the documents he had were altered to make the reader believe Clara Becker was a traitor. He had been outwitted in his own story, and knew he was a pawn in a game he could only lose.

The complete story, exposed on the table at the Bobst Library, proved that it was Ryan Burr who was the traitor attempting to cover his tracks. The NSA had uncovered proof of the cover-up, and was planning to alert the House Committee overseeing Homeland Security. Clara Becker's name was only recorded in the report as a member of the Committee. The creative editing of the first document implicated Clara as the person in question by the use of heavy redaction. Now, the entire falsified story was out and spreading like a plague. Malcolm and Ryan Burr had set him up, and the genie could not be coaxed back in the bottle. Malcolm had covered their tracks and manipulated the situation with precision. They knew Carson would be unable to retract the story, given his already unstable reputation. It was a perfect setup, and Carson was the perfect fall guy.

The
BACKLASH

Demonstrations outside the government building in D.C. were not uncommon. On any given day, citizens exhibited their First Amendment right to free speech with full conviction. Today's demonstration was different. For the first time since she took office, Clara Becker was the target of the protests. The backlash had begun as soon as the online story broke in the early hours, long before the daily media cycle began. Like sharks smelling fresh blood in the water, a line of satellite trucks flanked Independence Avenue as they prepared for the morning primetime reports. The one certainty of the national media was that they would give a controversial story legs, regardless of the quality of facts. Using the misleading intro, "According to sources…," was a clever way to report the story while leaving a vague escape clause should the story turn sour. Publishing an article alleging treasonous charges was a goldmine on its own. Implicating a United States congresswoman all but solidified a momentous distribution—and a healthy ratings boost.

From her office inside the Longworth Building, Clara thoughtfully peered out the window. Sara stood silently as the congresswoman gathered her thoughts. "Sara, can you tell me the purpose of this office?" Clara asked, observing the protestors below.

"Sure. You have taught us from the very beginning our purpose is to serve our constituents and the citizens of this country with honor," Sara replied.

"And, in your opinion, have we done that?" Clara asked.

"Yes ma'am. And then some, I would say."

Clara turned to face Sara and walked toward the center of her office. "As a lawmaker, I have learned to respect the process of our government. We aren't always perfect, but the process works when executed well. In my own life, I have also discovered a series of choices that have provided the guardrails on my journey." She took a seat on the sofa in front of her desk and motioned to Sara to have a seat in the chair across from her. "When you serve others with honor, you can always hold your head high," she instructed, leaning forward in her chair. Sara nodded her head in agreement, fully engaged in a teaching moment she knew would have a profound impact on her future.

A staff member knocked on the door to let Clara know that the Speaker of the House was on the phone. Clara reached over to the side table next to the sofa, picked up the headset, and spoke, "Mr. Speaker, how can I be of service?" Quietly Clara listened as the Speaker responded. After a very brief moment, Sara could see Clara's eyes begin to tear up. She quickly regained composure. "Thank you, Mr. Speaker. That means a great deal to me." After listening to his response, she hung up the phone. Looking over at Sara, who had not moved a muscle, Clara wiped her eyes. "When you live your life in the light of integrity, it becomes easier to see the truth when times get dark." Sara knew at that moment the Speaker had called to privately offer support to Clara. Now it was up to her to deal with the media.

Sara inspected her phone for the latest updates. "I would recommend not making a statement until we can find out more about the information in the article," Sara said.

"Nonsense," Clara said sharply. "We have nothing to hide and have done nothing wrong. I am worried for Carson," she said softly. Sara quickly looked up from her phone to make eye contact with Clara.

"After what he did to you, how can you possibly be worried about Carson? You are the name being protested on the street, not Carson Stewart. He is probably prepping for his first media cycle of interviews," Sara said without taking a breath.

"Sara, if we know what he wrote was untrue, then he had to be fed that information. Carson is a reporter, not a fiction writer. Kyle warned us something like this was looming," Clara reminded her. A steady flow of staffers brought a never-ending stream of messages from the media requesting an interview from Clara. Additionally, calls had begun filling the House switchboard asking for hearings into the allegations against the congresswoman. The backlash had begun, and it was only a few hours after the article had been uploaded online.

Sara moved with extreme poise throughout the office suite while she directed staffer traffic, frequently glancing to check for updates on her phone. One message stopped her in her tracks. It was from Carson. Opening the message, Sara stood perfectly still as she read the words, *"I've made a mistake. Please forgive me and let me try to explain."* She pushed the button to darken the screen and placed the phone on her desk. Fighting back tears, she focused on the media crisis brewing on the street below.

Perfectly timing the evening news cycle, Sara had scheduled a live press conference on the steps of the Capitol Building. The Capitol Police had constructed a barricade to keep the throng of people at a distance. The message and backdrop of the press conference was deliberately orchestrated. Clara would step to the podium and make a statement. Avoiding the prepared remarks Sara urged her to read, Clara convinced her that speaking from the heart was the mark of a true leader, as it demonstrated vulnerability and transparency. These were the qualities that Clara knew were missing from inside the Beltway.

Each media outlet set up cameras, making a semicircle around the congresswoman and her staff. The podium was covered with a multitude of recording devices set to capture Clara Becker's every word. As Clara began to speak, an extended roar came from the area around the barricades. A man dressed in olive-colored tactical pants, a black jacket, and cap jumped the barricade and began a full sprint towards the press conference. Reaching behind his back, he produced a semi-automatic 1911 .45 pistol and pointed it straight in front of him. Firing what appeared to be five rounds in quick succession, he suddenly came to an abrupt stop, collapsing like a ragdoll 30 yards from the congresswoman and the media.

The Capitol Police immediately secured the area and summoned additional protection as they placed the building on lockdown. First responders rushed to the crowd gathered on the Capitol steps. A Fox News cameraman writhed on the ground with a bullet through his right calf. Crouching behind the podium, Clara Becker had been struck in the hand and was checking for further wounds when she noticed Sara lying on the ground. The first EMT to make it to Clara asked where she was hit. Without hesitation, she yelled at him to check on Sara first. The EMT's insistence to first attend to the congresswoman prompted the full wrath of Clara. Within seconds, additional responders were on the scene attending to the potential casualties. Clara made her way to Sara who had been turned over to reveal a single gunshot wound to her left shoulder. Clara looked in desperate horror at the unconscious body of Sara Davis lying in a pool of blood.

A portion of the shooting was captured on camera by one of the news outlets. After careful review, the initial report of five shots fired by the killer was retracted to confirm he had only fired three shots. One of the remaining two shots heard on tape was the shot that was fired at the killer, taking him down. The Capitol police report also confirmed that the shot, which took down the potential assassin, was not fired from their squad. The mysterious fifth shot was confirmed when a body with a fatal gunshot wound was removed from a van nearby. The deceased was a known assassin from South America who had been wanted in the States, traveling on a falsified passport. The police reported that the running shooter was a distraction, while a trained terrorist took aim at his target. Thankfully, a single gunshot to the side of the head ended his mission to kill Clara Becker.

Reports of the assassination attempt dominated the next several news cycles. Speculation swirled around the identity and motivation of the running shooter. Immediately, the media concluded the entire incident was connected in someway to the scandal involving Clara Becker. Once again, the media was nowhere close to the truth, but for Malcolm Claire they were right on point. As Carson slowly grasped his role in the unfolding drama, his world began crashing down around him.

Clara stood over Sara's hospital bed, watching her sleep. After skilled doctors removed the bullet fragment from her shoulder, Sara was still under heavy anesthesia. Her mom was in route to D.C., on board a private jet provided by Kyle Ellis. Doctors moved in and out of the ICU at George Washington Hospital, ensuring Sara Davis received the best care. Clara's left arm was in a sling, protecting her freshly bandaged hand. Although she was hit by a clean, pass-through gunshot, she would also require surgery. Clara insisted the procedure could wait until she knew Sara was going to be fine.

Slipping out of the room for a brief moment, Clara made her way down the hall to ICU room six. A weary woman in her midforties sat in a chair holding the hand of the man in bed. The patient, Leonard Scott, was awake with his left leg elevated by a series of cables and pulleys. He was having a conversation with his wife, Marla, who was the first to notice Clara as she entered the room.

"I didn't want to disturb you. Just wanted to check on how you are recovering," Clara said with a soft voice, as she stood just inside the sliding glass doorway. "I'm Clara Becker," she continued.

"We know who you are, ma'am," Leonard replied.

"Please come in," Marla said, as she stood to formally greet Clara. "Thank you for stopping by. The surgery went well—they removed the bullet from just below the knee. He will be out for awhile but thankfully will survive." Marla offered with relief in her voice.

"Thank the Lord," Clara replied.

"Ma'am, can I ask why you are here?" Leonard said with a raspy voice.

"I wanted to make sure you were okay, young man," Clara offered with a reassuring smile.

"Thank you, ma'am, but you realize I was there broadcasting your conference to report the scandal you are involved in," Leonard said, his honesty fueled by the pain medication he was on at the moment.

"I know why you were there," Clara said. "You were just doing your job," she smiled and continued, "The FBI briefed me a few hours ago and told me the only video of the shooter came from your camera. Seems that while everyone else hit the ground, you decided to turn toward the gunfire. I certainly appreciate someone with that much passion for what they do," she offered, now standing alongside Leonard's bed.

Marla was quick to jump in, "I would be fine with a little less passion." The comment brought a much-needed moment of laughter to the room.

"Leonard, you are a brave and committed person. Thank you for what you do and the service you have provided our country," Clara said. "The FBI also gave me your background.

They informed me you served three tours of duty in the Middle East. I appreciate your service deeply," she continued. Not wanting to wear Leonard out, she gently squeezed Leonard's hand and turned to head back to Sara's side.

Marla placed her hand on Clara's shoulder and whispered, "Thank you."

Before Clara was able to reach the door, Leonard spoke, "How is the young lady who was shot?"

"She just came out of surgery and the report is promising. Many prayers are with her. Thank you for asking," Clara replied as she hastened out the door to check on Sara.

The
TRAGEDY

It had been over a week since Joe had seen Carson. Repeated attempts to reach him via phone and text brought no response. There had been no follow-up article as promised in Carson's first installment, which prompted a call to Joe from Brian. "Any chance you have seen Carson?" Brian asked. "No sightings for over a week," Joe responded.

"Well, he missed his deadline and now all hell is breaking loose over here," Brian said with a slightly elevated voice.

"The deadline may be the least of our worries," Joe said as he ended the call abruptly. With the phone still in his hand, Joe swiped through his contacts until he located the name he needed. An old friend in the NYPD agreed to do a welfare check on Carson. Within minutes, a unit had been dispatched to Carson's apartment to check on his status.

Joe's phone alerted him to an incoming call from his friend at the NYPD. "We found your friend," the officer said.

"Alive?" Joe asked, his heart pounding in his head.

"Unresponsive. FDNY just rushed him to Sinai," came the response.

"Appreciate the update," Joe said as he tapped to end the call. A quick text message to bring in backup bar help allowed Joe the ability to make his way to Mount Sinai Hospital. Waiting for his backup to arrive, Joe sent a text to Brian with the update on Carson. The message received a quick reply stating Brian would be en route to the hospital also. Before walking out the door, Joe sent one additional text to an old friend who also needed to be kept in the loop.

The ER doctors moved quickly, assessing Carson's situation. The attending doctor had already made note of the strong smell of alcohol. The blue-tinged skin color accompanied by the low body temperature led to an initial diagnosis of alcohol poisoning. The still-unconscious Carson Stewart's life was now in the hands of the medical team who began treatment immediately.

When Joe arrived, he met his friend with the NYPD outside the ER doors. "Thanks for checking on him," Joe extended his hand to the officer, clenching his in a strong, emotional grip.

"No worries, brother. Glad you called when you did. Another hour and he would have been gone. We found him with four empties," the officer gave the facts without softening the details. Joe stood in disbelief at the information. "Docs are trying to stabilize him now," the officer continued.

It would be two days before Carson regained consciousness. The full extent of the damage would not be diagnosed for several more days. Carson opened his eyes to a blurry, unknown room. Not knowing or understanding what was going on, his first response was to lunge forward. The force from the straps restraining him quickly forced him back into his bed. The tube in his throat was placed there to assist in breathing, but now was preventing him from speaking. The panic which ensued elevated his heart rate enough to set off the monitor, summoning a nurse into the room rapidly. "Good to have you back, Mr. Carson," the nurse said as she alerted the on-call doctor that Carson was awake. She knew Carson wasn't out of the woods just yet.

The name on Clara Becker's phone prompted a deliberate reaction. "Clara, it's Kyle," said the strained voice on the other end.

"Have you learned anything new?" Clara cut in with a burst of energy.

"We have a solid lead we are following currently. I'm calling for another reason. Clara, Carson Stewart is in critical condition in Mount Sinai," Kyle explained. The phone remained silent as Clara processed the new information.

"Foul play?" she asked.

"Not likely, considering the four empty bottles of whiskey they found in his room. Looks like he may have been trying to drink himself to death," Kyle said, knowing Clara would need a moment to process the news. Clara closed her eyes to say a quick prayer, then spoke.

"How did you find him?" she asked.

"Mac got a tip from an old friend," Kyle explained. "Seems the friend's call to the authorities saved Carson's life." Clara's eyes became moist as she listened to the report from Kyle.

"The last twenty-four hours have been a terrible tragedy, but Carson unquestionably has a guardian angel watching over him. So do Sara and I, for that matter. Let me know when he is well enough for visitors. It appears I need to have a chat with that young man!" Clara exclaimed.

"Will do. And when I get confirmation on our lead, I will send you an update." Clara ended the call and said another prayer for young Carson Stewart.

The
REDEMPTION

For hospital food, her meal wasn't bad. Sara enjoyed being able to order from a menu at any time of the day, now that she was in a private room. The last report from the doctor gave her hope she would be going home in the morning. Next week would begin several weeks of physical therapy on her shoulder. She would fly back to Dallas by the end of the week to finish recovering with support from her mom. Clara insisted on having a full-time nurse assigned to look after Sara, but Sara promptly declined. Sara's support network in Dallas was strong, and she was confident her recovery would go well with the help of friends and family.

Clara never missed a day visiting Sara during her stay in the hospital. "I hear the doctor is setting you free in the morning," Clara declared in a booming voice as she entered the room. "This is great news!" she continued. Coming alongside Sara's bed, Clara reached out to hold Sara's hand as she did each and every day, her gentle squeeze reassuring her it would be okay. Today however, Clara held on a bit longer.

"Sweetie, there is something I have been waiting to tell you," Clara began. "The day after the shooting, the police found Carson nearly dead in his apartment. He is still in the hospital, but reports tell me he should recover." Sara looked at Clara silently. The pressure of Sara's grip on Clara's hand increased ever so slightly as she tried to form words to say. "I know what you are thinking. There was no foul play. He tried to kill himself with alcohol," Clara continued. By now a single tear had made its way down the crest of Sara's cheek. "I wanted you to know, but needed you strong enough to process the information," Clara explained. "I am flying up to New York City for a couple of days, and plan to visit him while I'm there. He and I have some things to discuss."

The look in Sara's eyes spoke louder than any words. "We have made a few important discoveries during your stay in the hospital," Clara began. "First, we learned Carson was set up to write the article. He was given falsified information and led to believe it was the truth."

"What information?" Sara asked, speaking her first words of the visit.

"We found the documents he used. For some reason, he felt no one would look for them in the freezer," Clara said in a lighthearted manner, lifting the mood.

"What are you going to say to him?" Sara asked, still clinging to Clara's hand.

"Simple. That we know he was misled and I forgive him," Clara said without hesitation.

"But he made a choice—a terrible choice," Sara said.

"Yes, sweetie, we all make choices. And he made his. The consequences of those choices will continue to play out over time and neither of us can wipe that away. My role is not to judge, but to forgive," Clara said.

"That is much easier said than done. The betrayal and hurt is deep," Sara said, trying to be strong.

"A key lesson of life for me, sweetie, is that choosing to lead with love has a longer shelf life than choosing to lead with judgment," Clara explained. "Love is the one thing that will set both parties free."

"We are going to miss you, Mr. Stewart," the hospital orderly commented as he helped Carson into the wheelchair.

"No offense, but I'm not going to miss this place," Carson replied, as he gently lowered himself into the chair. It took just a few minutes for Carson to be pushed to the lower level exit of the hospital. During the ride, he had time to reflect on the last week he spent recovering from his near-death experience. The papers resting in his lap were just one reminder of his stay. As an unemployed journalist, the bill for his stay in the hospital was enough to create additional stress, which was exactly the opposite of what the doctor advised.

"Do you have someone picking you up, Mr. Stewart?" asked the young man.

"No. I'm just going to grab a cab home," Carson replied as the wheelchair rolled through the sliding doors. Once outside the hospital, a gentleman dressed in a black suit and wearing dark sunglasses greeted the two men.

"Mr. Stewart?" the gentleman inquired.

"Yes, and who are you?" Carson asked suspiciously. With one fluid motion the man in black reached for the rear door of a black SUV, replying, "Your ride, sir. Please get in."

Carson sat frozen as his still-recovering mind tried to process the current events. "That beats a cab any day of the week, Mr. Stewart!" came a joyous response from the hospital orderly. Slowly, Carson pushed up out of the wheelchair to move with guarded caution towards the opened door of the suburban.

When he reached the door, he heard a familiar voice calling from inside, "Hello, Carson. You are looking well."

Carson stopped dead in his tracks as he came eye-to-eye with Clara Becker. The same woman who he tried to ruin, and who had endured an assassination attempt as a result of his article, was now offering him a ride. His first thought was to turn and walk away but he could sense the insistence of the man in black, and he was really in no condition to walk very far anyway. Slowly he stepped into the back seat, feeling his heart rate begin to elevate. The door closed behind him and the man in black climbed into the front passenger seat. Silently, Carson sat back as the car pulled away from the hospital. Fatigued from his recovery, Carson tried his best to relax, given the current situation.

Clara broke the awkward silence first. "Sara sends her best wishes," she began. The thought of Sara sent shooting pains of shame throughout Carson's weak body.

"How is she?" came the shaky response from Carson.

"She is healing nicely. She will spend a few weeks in Texas recovering," Clara replied. Remembering the destructive outcome of his words left Carson speechless and ashamed. "I thought we could grab a bite to eat. A week of hospital food must have you craving some of the City's finest," Clara offered as the SUV turned toward Midtown.

The next several blocks were filled with awkward silence as the two rode without speaking. Finally, the suburban pulled to the side of the road and both men in black exited the vehicle to open the rear doors. Carson had not been paying attention during the ride, and realized upon stepping out of the vehicle that they were now in Central Park. "Come, I promised you some real food. I know who has the best dog in the city," Clara said with a bright smile. Carson couldn't help but smile also, incredulous that this woman would want to dine with him. The two walked slowly along the path in the Park, flanked by the bodyguards the entire stroll.

"Life must feel like a hot mess right about now," Clara began.

"That would be an understatement," Carson quietly replied. Approaching the hot dog cart, Clara looked at Carson playfully.

"What will you have on your dog?"

"The works," Carson said with a hint of a smile.

"Make that two," she said to the man behind the cart. With the speed of a master craftsman, the street vendor produced two dogs and drinks in a blink. "Let's grab a bench by the fountain," Clara said. Together, they walked down the few flights of stairs to the Bethesda Fountain and found a seat along the outside edge, the men in black never far away.

"Thank you for the hot dog," Carson said as he stuffed the first bite of real food into his mouth in over a week. His ability to keep food down had been somewhat limited in the first few days of his recovery.

"You are welcome," came the reply from Clara.

Midway through his hotdog, Carson paused to ask, "I need to know why you are doing this, ma'am."

"I thought you could use some help," Clara replied, still working her way through her hotdog while trying her best not to make a mess.

Still holding his hotdog in midair, Carson responded, "But why would you want to help me?"

"Well, young man, it's like this. We found the fake papers and have an idea about where they came from. I believe you were set up and made a bad choice. Heck, we all make bad choices from time to time. It seems to be part of what makes us human," Clara added. "I believe, deep inside you is a brilliant journalist who needs to recognize his true potential."

Carson sat listening to Clara in disbelief. The woman he tried to ruin was telling *him* he had potential. Maybe the medication from the hospital was creating some sort of hallucination, because he couldn't wrap his mind around such kindness. Clara continued, "Don't misunderstand, what you did was wrong and there are consequences for your actions. Some of those consequences have played out against innocent people." Carson immediately thought of Sara. The one person with whom he had developed a budding relationship was put directly into harm's way—not to mention the cameraman who was also shot. Carson completely lost his appetite for the last bite of his hotdog.

"Even though what you did was wrong and people got hurt, you need to know I forgive you," Clara continued. Carson was stunned by what he was hearing and struggled to speak without his voice cracking.

"But why?" he managed to ask.

"Years ago, someone forgave me and paid a costly price in doing so. Never asked for anything in return, either. Just did it out of love. Ever since then I have committed to a life purpose to do the same," Clara said. "I set out to lead with love as I fulfill this purpose for the people of Texas and the country. Wouldn't be much of a leader if I said one thing, and did something else, now would I?" she said with a little wink.

Carson used what was left of the white napkin from the hotdog cart to dry the tears rolling down his cheeks. "It might be the medication, but I don't understand why," he said.

"Carson, some people are good and end up doing stupid things often because they are wandering through life without purpose. Without purpose, choices become difficult," she began. "There are evil people in the world. Let's not be naive about that. Evil people will continue to do evil acts and we should work to stop evil from happening to innocent people. The jury was out on you, until Sara convinced me you were a good person. She saw something in you that others have not seen—potential. It is a fulfilling day when those you have been mentoring begin to teach you. Sara caused me to remember my own purpose and what I stand for," Clara said, before pausing to finish off the last bite of her hotdog.

Carson sat staring at the magnificent fountain before him as he took in what he had just heard. "I don't know what to say," Carson said.

"Sweetie, there isn't anything for you to say right now," Clara said.

"Do you think she will ever be able to forgive me?" Carson asked.

"That is not mine to answer," Clara replied, "but why don't you ask her yourself?"

Clara pointed up the stairs to a railing overlooking the fountain. There, standing with her arm in a sling, was Sara. Slowly she raised her hand to wave when Carson made eye contact. The unsure look on her face gradually turned into a full smile as she watched Carson sprinting up the stairs to join her. Arriving at the top of the stairs, he stopped in full view of the one person who made his heart race. With a steady stream of tears rolling down his face, he deliberately walked closer to Sara. Without taking his eyes off hers, he spoke. "Can you ever forgive me?" Seeing the tears in Carson's eyes prompted Sara's blue eyes to blur with tears also.

"Yes, Carson, I forgive you," she said with kindness and sincerity. Carson gently leaned over, and with a perfectly soft touch, kissed Sara on the cheek.

From below, Clara watched the reunion and smiled. Her bodyguard appeared out of nowhere. "Ready to go, ma'am?" he asked.

"Yes," she replied, as she rose from the bench. "Kyle will be expecting us soon." She headed back to the SUV. Stopping to look back at Sara and Carson for a brief moment prompted a protective response from her detail.

"Everything okay, ma'am?" he asked, stopping to scan the surrounding area for anything suspicious.

"Yes. Everything is more than okay. It seems Carson is going to make the choice that will change his life forever," Clara stated, with a pleased smile.

"And what choice is that, ma'am?" her guard was still wondering if the area was secured.

"Carson chose redemption, finally. Make sure all his medical bills are taken care of. I want him to have a fresh start. No one needs to know I paid them," she said as she disappeared into the back seat.

"Understood, ma'am," he replied, as he shut the back door on one of the most satisfying lunches in Clara's career.

The
PLAN

The ride up the art deco elevator to the offices of Kyle
Ellis was one Clara had made several times during their long
friendship. Today's trip to Ellis International's world headquarters was certainly a departure from their normal casu-
al meetings. The expansive suite atop the midtown high-rise
provided breathtaking views of the City. Kyle immediately
greeted Clara as she emerged from the elevator.

"Clara, it so great to see you. How did this morning go?"
Kyle asked.

"Very promising," Clara replied.

"Can I offer you a cup of coffee or maybe a Diet Coke
to finishing washing down the Park dog I know you just
consumed?" Kyle inquired with a smile.

"Diet Coke would be great. Thank you." Clara retreated
to the seating area in the middle of Kyle's office. "How are we
coming on the balance of the plan?" she asked as Kyle walked
up with a glass of her favorite soft drink in hand.

"We seem to be on track. I am waiting to hear back from Mac on one detail and we should be ready to go," Kyle replied as he sat in the tufted leather chair across from Clara.

"We have offered Ryan Burr the opportunity to come clean, but, as predicted, he is denying any connection to the incident," Kyle began. "He claims we have no proof, with the exception of some washed-up, alcoholic journalist out to make a name for himself."

"So he doesn't know about the file?" Clara asked, sipping her drink while assessing their plan.

"It appears not." Kyle said, putting his drink on the table.

"Where is Malcolm in all this?" Clara inquired.

"Surprisingly cooperative," Kyle said reassuringly. Clara smiled.

"One thing is always certain about a person who has no integrity—they are predictable to a fault when it comes to protecting their own hide."

Mac entered the massive office unnoticed by Clara. After years of working with Mac, Kyle was one of the few people able to sense when he silently entered a room. Without turning around, Kyle asked, "What did you find out, Mac?" Clara looked up to find her old friend standing just feet away. Jumping to her feet, she gave Mac a huge hug. "I don't remember getting a hug like that when you came in," Kyle said with a snicker.

"Nonsense, you always get hugs. It was the smell of hotdog that kept you at a distance this time. Now then, what *did* you find out, Mac?" Clara asked.

The three sat down as Mac began, "Our contact at the NSA confirms the file was downloaded from an unauthorized computer."

"Someone hacked the NSA?" Clara exclaimed.

"Not just someone, but a level-one black hat," Mac continued. Kyle smiled at the information.

"And why are you smiling?" Clara asked Kyle, looking back and forth between the two.

Mac and Kyle looked at each other and simultaneously answered, "Susan Hall."

Clara couldn't help but smile and in a very soft voice asked, "And who is Susan Hall?"

Kyle explained, "Ms. Hall is an old friend we helped out a few years back. She is an incredibly gifted programmer who made some bad choices. She was given a second chance and has used her skills to do amazing things for good."

"And how does she help us?" Clara asked.

Mac responded, "It seems the hacker they used to steal the documents from the NSA was sloppy and left a trail of sorts. Susan not only found the trail, but also located the hacker. Susan shut him down just as NSA agents were busting down his door. He promptly rolled over on who hired him."

"And?" Clara asked now sitting on the side of the sofa.

"It was just as we expected," Mac continued, "Malcolm Claire."

The three sat quietly for a moment to let the name sink in. Clara spoke first, "Is there proof?"

"According to Susan, once she got into the hacker's computer there was proof on the NSA hack and much more. All of it linked back to Ryan Burr," Mac explained.

"This is the confirmation we needed in order to continue as planned," Kyle said.

"Yes, I agree. We continue as planned. If Ryan Burr refuses to come clean on his own, then I will schedule a meeting with the head of the FBI," Clara resolved.

"What are the odds he does the right thing?" Kyle asked.

"Historically, people lacking integrity and honor and will always default to protecting self over others," Mac offered.

"Well, we made Malcolm the same offer. Let's see if he chooses our offer of redemption, or continues down his own path." Clara finished her drink and shook both men's hands in agreement.

The
LIFE LESSONS

The last time Carson walked through the door to *Joe's Place* was the night he made his misguided choice. Slightly nervous to face his old friend, he pulled the door open and walked in, mentally preparing himself for a verbal onslaught. Within a few steps he heard a familiar, friendly greeting. "Hello, Carson," Joe announced. Walking to his old spot at the bar, Carson extended his hand to Joe. In all the years Carson had been coming into *Joe's Place*, never once did he offer to shake Joe's hand.

Without asking, Joe poured Carson a mineral water and slid it across the bar top. Both men began to smile and nod their heads while looking at the drink. At 2 o'clock in the afternoon the bar was always quiet. Picking up the glass and offering a toast in the air, Carson took a long drink of the ice-cold beverage.

"Great to see you again," Joe began, his voice cracking slightly.

"Likewise," Carson said, putting down his glass.

"You gave us a scare, old friend," Joe added. Carson nodded in agreement without saying a word.

After finishing his mineral water Carson finally spoke. "I owe you an apology, Joe," he began.

"And why is that, Carson?" Joe asked.

"You tried to help me that night I was wrestling with my decision, and I refused to listen," Carson replied. "I was stubborn, foolish, and just plain wrong. I should have listened to you."

"Apology accepted," Joe replied, thoughtfully looking him over. "I guess my next question is going to be, what's your new story?" He looked Carson directly in the eyes.

"What do you mean, my new story?" Carson asked, trying to process the question and squirming a bit under Joe's steady gaze.

"Life teaches us lessons every day, by way of the information we take in. We then apply that information through the choices we make, which in turn creates experiences. It is those experiences that develop our story, which subsequently transforms our life. Our ability to know and understand those stories increases our effectiveness in the future, and gives us the ability to recognize and avoid repeated mistakes," Joe began. "Don't miss the importance of your recent struggles. Our struggles in life can provide insightful meaning to our story," he emphasized.

"So, again, what is your new story going to be?" he asked with laser focus.

Carson pondered the question for a few moments as Joe poured him another mineral water. "I've recently been given a second chance," Carson reflected, still wondering how Clara was led to be so gracious to him.

"What does that mean to you?" Joe asked, searching his face for an answer.

"I guess I'm still working that part out," Carson replied, straining to grasp the new lease on life he had been afforded.

"Let me ask you a question," Joe said. "A year ago, when you were still writing your syndicated column, when someone asked you what you did, what was your answer?"

"I would tell them I wrote an award-winning, nationally syndicated column," Carson responded without missing a beat.

"And when that came crashing down around you, what did you tell people?" Joe asked.

"That's easy. I didn't tell people anything, because I avoided them at all costs," Carson said, now able to at least crack a smile about that season of his life.

"So can you see the connection? For years, you attached your self-worth to your position within your job. Once that was gone, so was your self-worth," Joe offered, hoping Carson was absorbing the wisdom of his words.

Carson began sipping the freshly poured drink, seeking to provide much-needed moisture to his dry mouth. Joe's words made a great deal of sense. Without his title and position, Carson felt he was no one. Yes, the guilt of his professional mistakes was overwhelming, but when he really contemplated the events of his past, it was the feelings of shame and failure that far outdistanced the feeling of guilt. For Carson, his position in life was everything, and each choice he made was focused on advancing his career, regardless of the cost to others. On the other side of town, it was this same fateful outlook that was about to bring down another member of the House of Representatives—Ryan Burr. Carson definitely did not want to be the byline on that news story.

The
DINER

"So help me understand something," Carson said.

"Name it," Joe quickly replied, fully embracing this new depth in their relationship.

"How do I avoid ruining this second chance to write a new story?" Carson asked, with the sincerity of the college student who first walked in his door years ago.

"Your story is being written as we speak," Joe replied. "You just need to take the time to understand what you are learning as each page unfolds. Think about your last two weeks. Tell me the theme that is running through everything you have experienced," he prodded. Carson closed his eyes tightly in an effort to draw all the details of the last few weeks to the forefront of his memory.

"There seems to be three themes around a central storyline," Carson began. "The themes are: loving, forgiving, and serving."

"And what would be the main storyline?" Joe asked, nodding his head with approval.

"The storyline could be that true meaning in life comes from making these three choices with purpose," Carson said with a hint of understanding. Joe restrained a slight smile as he recognized Carson's budding excitement.

"Some would call those the three choices of a meaningful life," Joe said with a steady tone in his voice. "This is a great start, my friend. This food for thought calls for some food in the stomach. Let's go get some lunch!" he declared. "I know just the place. Help me lock up while I change the kegs in the basement." Joe threw the ever-present white towel over his right shoulder while turning towards the stairs.

"But aren't you about to open?" Carson asked with a puzzled look.

"No worries, you are the only person who ever shows up at this hour," Joe said with a chuckle as he headed toward the back stairway leading to the basement. "You will find the keys to the front door in the drawer. Lock up, turn the sign off, and I will meet you by the back door," he instructed.

Joe headed down the narrow stairs while Carson made his way around to the back of the bar. In all the years he had been coming to *Joe's Place*, this was Carson's first time behind the bar. Carson began pulling out drawers looking for the keys to the front door. Opening what appeared to be the classic junk drawer of the bar, two small, leather-clad boxes trimmed in gold caught Carson's eye. He quietly looked up to see if Joe was still downstairs. He reached into the crowded drawer to extract one of the two boxes. On top of the box were two words, *Silver Star*. The other box was also engraved with two words, *Purple Heart*. Slowly opening the box, Carson pulled out a star-shaped, gold medal of honor, draped with a red, white, and blue ribbon. Carson couldn't believe what he cradling in his hands.

Hearing Joe make his way up the back staircase, Carson quickly replaced the medals in the drawer, located the keys, and made his way to lock the door just as Joe was appearing. "Ready?" Joe shouted from the rear of the bar. "Don't forget the light."

"Heading that way," Carson said as he pulled the beaded chain hanging from the flickering neon sign that illuminated the passing world outside the bar. In a matter of moments, the two were slipping out the back and into the ally leading to 6th Street.

"I know just the place," Joe began as he motioned in the direction they needed to go. "Best burger in the area," he continued as he headed out with military precision.

A short walk put them on a path towards the Meat Packing District in the city. "How well do you know your City history?" Joe asked as they navigated the ever-crowded streets.

"Fairly well. I've been here most of my life," Carson replied.

"What do you know about the Meat Packing District?" Joe asked.

"Well, mostly that they used to pack meat there a long time ago and now it is a hip and trendy part of the city," Carson replied, without much confidence in his voice. Joe smiled as the two came to a stop at the intersection of Greenwich Ave and 11th Street. Anticipating the light like true city dwellers, the two stepped into the street and joined the flow of pedestrian traffic.

"Interesting fact about this part of town," Joe began as they continued to walk. "These few blocks have gone through several changes in the last hundred years, some for the better, some for the worst. The early eighties were a dark time for this section of the city, with little-to-no development happening. A small group of people who cared about the city came together to change the story of this neighborhood. Now, like you acknowledged, it is one of the hottest spots in town," he explained. Carson began to grin as he realized the connection to the story.

"So, are you saying my life is much like the Meat Packing District?" Carson blurted out.

"Let's just say you have had your dark days and now you have the chance at restoration," Joe said in a jovial tone. They both began to laugh as they continued to walk toward their lunch destination.

Walking past the historic brick buildings along Gansevoort Street, they arrived at a corner establishment named *Bubby's*. "Best burger in the area!" Joe exclaimed again, as they settled into their seats inside the extraordinary building. "You have to try the *Double Bubby*," Joe stated with a childlike eagerness in his voice. Before Carson could respond, two glasses of water were being placed on the table accompanied by an undeniable Queens accent from the 40-something waitress now standing tableside.

"Morning, my name is Marisa and I am here to serve you today. Hey, Joe. Who is your cute friend?" she said, with an infectious tone in her voice. Her pace had been quick, determined, and efficient as she moved between the five tables in her section of the restaurant. While tableside, however, she never took her gaze off of Joe and Carson, giving them the full impression that they were the only people dining with her at that moment.

"Hi Marisa, I'm Carson. This is my first time here. Any recommendations?" Carson said while still studying the menu.

"Sweetie, if you are hungry, you have to try the *Double Bubby*," she replied, drawing a look of affirmation from Joe across the table. Placing his menu on the table, Carson looked up and smiled.

"It must be good, and I am hungry. I will have that."

"You won't be disappointed," she said as she scribbled a note on the small piece of paper she was holding.

"Make that two," Joe replied enthusiastically. With a grin, the waitress pivoted on one foot and disappeared to enter their order. "I've only been here twice and she remembered my name. I need to talk to her about working at the bar," Joe said, leaning on the table. "She could drive a ton of business. Did you notice how she connected with us in the short amount of time she was here? Remarkable, wouldn't you say?"

"Why would you say it is remarkable?" Carson asked. "Think about the experience she just created in a matter of minutes for both of us. What struck you immediately about her?" Joe asked.

"She remembered you and genuinely wanted to know about me," Carson said without much effort.

"Precisely. I can tell you from experience behind the bar, when you truly care about the person you're with, you connect quicker, creating a meaningful experience for both people. It confirms the statement you made before we left the bar about the three choices. The first choice was all about loving others," Joe explained.

"But isn't her job to be friendly to guests?" Carson asked innocently. The look on Joe's face was one of amusement.

"Ever eat at a restaurant in the city where they weren't friendly?" Joe said with a grin.

They both laughed as Carson replied, "Great point."

"So think about this for a moment. What would be different if you lead with love?" Joe asked as he sipped his water. Placing the glass on the table he continued, "After all, the alternative is to lead out of judgment. You have experienced both, so what have you learned?"

"Clara Becker and Sara have demonstrated something I have never experienced in my life. They showed an unconditional type of love for someone who has been the poster boy of unlovable. They had every reason to judge me, yet they showed me compassion," Carson confessed, still bewildered by their behavior.

Joe interjected for a moment, "Before I departed for Special Forces training, a wise person pulled me aside to give me counsel that has made a huge difference in my life." Carson's eyes widened as a small glimpse into the life of Joe Hamilton was revealed.

Carson asked, "And what was the counsel?"

Joe smiled as he continued, "She told me power without love leads to barbarism. The words stuck with me. No matter how powerful I became, if I didn't love others the same way I was loving myself, I would quickly slip into barbarism."

"That sounds a little extreme. How did that work, given your role in the military?" Carson asked, with a slightly puzzled look on his face.

Joe smiled. "That is a good question, Carson. I fought to protect those I loved from those who had resorted to total barbarism. My unit came face-to-face with people who had obtained some sort of power and their sole mission was to use it to destroy others who were different from them," Joe said with a solemn tone in his voice.

Carson's eyes began to tear up listening to Joe talk about his life. For the first time in over a decade, Carson was seeing a side of Joe he never knew existed. He couldn't help but wonder how many layers Joe would continue to unpeel. After a few moments, Carson finally spoke.

"So, if I am comprehending what you are saying correctly, Clara and Sara didn't do what they did merely out of spontaneity," he commented.

"That's correct," Joe said. "Everything they did was on purpose. You said it yourself, the path to true meaning in life comes from making these three choices with purpose," he explained. "You have already witnessed that in action. But don't be fooled into thinking making these choices is easy. Making these choices requires sacrifice. There is always something to be given up, and very few are willing to let go."

Joe could sense Carson contemplating his last comment. "I can see the wheels in your head spinning," Joe said. "You are wondering what do you need to give up in order to lead in the same manner as Clara and Sara. The answer is simple, just not easy. You have to give up self," he said with a matter-of-fact tone in his voice. Carson remained silent, pondering the impact of those words.

"There is something I know about the congresswoman; she has always lived her life on purpose," Joe continued. "It's her purpose in life that directed her to treat you the way she did. Her purpose is fueled by what she values most, serving others."

Carson jumped in, eyeing Joe suspiciously. "How can you know that?"

At that moment Marisa appeared with two plates. "Mr. Carson, I'm about to make you the happiest person in the city," she exclaimed as she placed the monstrous plate of food before Carson and Joe. Carson's face lit up with extreme excitement at the sight of the eight-inch-high mountain of burger before him. "Sweetie, I take you to be a ketchup guy," she said with a wide grin, as she produced a bottle from what seemed like thin air. Topping off Joe's water glass with one hand, she produced a thin stack of napkins with the other. "Here you go, Joe," she said, anticipating Joe's next request. Looking back at Carson, she said precociously, "Joe's a three napkin kinda guy." Giving a wink and grin, she placed a few extra napkins in front of Carson. "I think you might find these useful." She turned towards the kitchen and said, "I'm here for both of you. Just holler if you need something!" And with that, Marisa disappeared into the sea of guests.

Preparing his attack plan on the burger before him, Carson sat motionless, in awe of the colossal work of food art. "I don't know where to begin," he said.

Picking up his knife and fork first, Joe responded, "I have found hand-to-hand combat to be the best attack." He began carving up the mass of food like a special ops military surgeon.

Carson carefully began working his way through the multiple layers of his meal as he spoke. "You're not getting off the hook for the last question I asked," he said as he forked his first bite.

"That's a long story for another day. Just trust me on this one, Clara has been living on purpose for a long time," Joe offered as he dissected the *Double Bubby*. "When you know your purpose and live your life on purpose, your self-worth is no longer attached to your position or work. It becomes just the opposite. I would be willing to bet Marisa doesn't see her job as work, but more as a calling to connect. I have got to get her at the bar," he said under his breath while stabbing another bite.

"So how do I find my purpose?" Carson asked.

"That, my friend, is a great question. Chances are you already know it—you just haven't embraced it for what it is," Joe said, pointing the empty end of his fork towards Carson.

"Your purpose is why you are here," Joe elaborated with a smile, exploring this new idea for Carson. "Everyone has a purpose. Think of purpose as a journey to someplace deliberate. You're a journalist, so think of it more like a verb instead of a noun."

"Okay, I can work with that, now that you put it in those terms," Carson replied.

Joe continued, "For me, to find my purpose, I needed to examine my life. The questions I asked myself were: What are my gifts and talents, and what do I really value most? When these two areas of my life came together in a way to serve others, it became clear why I was here. I began to understand my purpose."

Carson wrestled with his words along with the stack of dismembered food before him and asked, "Okay, I seem to have a gift for writing and telling stories, so is that it?" Joe smiled as he watched his friend embrace this shift in his life.

"That's a start," Joe began. "There are a couple of things missing. Two words that will help you bring it all together: *others* and *significance*."

Just then, Marisa appeared. "How well is that burger treating you?" She asked while refilling both glasses of water.

Carson looked up from his plate, which now resembled nothing close to a burger.

"This is perfect," he said with a smile.

Joe looked up with a grin, "Marisa, I have a question for you."

"Anything, sweetie," she replied, pausing and crossing her arms.

"What's your story? Why do you work here?" he asked.

"That's easy, Joe. I get to feed people's hunger for food and for life," she said with a look of great satisfaction. "I used to work for the money only, then realized how unhappy I was. There was just no joy in that, in fact, it felt like drudgery. Then I recognized what fulfilled me was helping others have a more fulfilled day, both literally and figuratively. When I stopped focusing on the money and started focusing on the people, I ended up making more money than I ever made in my life."

Joe couldn't help himself when he asked, "Ever consider running a bar?" The question caused Carson to almost choke on his next bite of fries.

Marisa smiled and replied, "Always interested in new adventures, darlin'." With that, she turned to delight the next guest in her section.

Joe used his fork as a conductor directs the symphony. "She figured it out. I found out the hard way," he said, smiling as he watched Marisa effortlessly work the dining room.

"Figured out what?" Carson asked mid bite.

"When I focused only on myself, the world became empty and meaningless. I looked for anything to fill the void. For me, I turned to the bottle to numb those feelings of worthlessness. We all reach for different vices to fill the vacuum, but one thing is the same for everyone—a life focused only on self is a life filled with empty joy. You heard her, there was no joy in working only for the money, it was empty," Joe said as carved the remains of his burger.

"What do you mean by *empty joy?*" Carson asked.

"In school did you ever read a book by Viktor Frankl?" Joe probed.

"If I did, I don't remember it," Carson confessed as he still slashed away at the food on his plate.

"Frankl wrote a book in 1945 that explained what he discovered during the war from inside a concentration camp. He wrote that the primary quest in life is to find meaning. For him, he found three possible sources of meaning in our life: our work, our love, and our courage. He discovered that we all want to do something of significance in our life. Carson, this is what we really value. So, empty joy is a life devoid of what we really value; it's missing significance. It's a fleeting moment of euphoria that once passed, leaves you empty and in despair." Carson sat stunned at Joe's words, and yet it made perfect sense as he reflected on his life.

"So I know when I am living on purpose, I will find joy as I use my gifts and talents in a way to serve others?" Carson tentatively asked.

"Nailed it," Joe replied. "Remember though, it's a journey. True joy comes from living a meaningful life on purpose, measured by steps, not miles."

Carson ate as much as he could handle, and pushed the plate of remaining food away from the edge of the table. "I'm beyond full," he proclaimed. Instantly, Marisa appeared to remove the plate.

"You did so well. Proud of you! Most first timers tap out much earlier," she said with a jovial tone.

"Marisa, this has been a delightful experience. Thank you," Carson complimented someone serving him for the first time in recent memory.

"Thank you, Carson. That means a great deal to me," she replied with sincerity. Joe finished his last bite and handed his empty plate to Marisa as she stood tableside. "Now there is a *Double Bubby* veteran," she said as all three laughed at Joe's clean plate.

The
BAR

Carson made his way to *Joe's Place*. The mid-afternoon walk through the streets of the Village was filled with a never-ending array of sights, sounds, and smells. Carson began noticing elements of the city he had overlooked, now that his head was clear and focused. His pace was brisk as he navigated the side streets, greeting people for the first time. These were the same people he had seen before, but had been ignoring for years. The bewildered look on their faces would become commonplace for Carson as he embraced his new persona.

Arriving a *Joe's*, he pulled the door open and entered what felt like his second home. "Hey sweetie, welcome to *Joe's*!" came a distinct voice from behind the bar. Only this wasn't the familiar voice of Joe. Allowing his eyes to momentarily adjust to the dim light, Carson slowly began to focus on the person who bellowed the greeting. There, in the place Joe had stood all these years, was Marisa, busy pulling a draft beer for a guest sitting at the bar.

Carson stood in disbelief for a brief moment, allowing the shift in his world to settle in. Instantly, Joe's voice broke Carson's trance.

"Relax, I'm still here. Meet my future bar manager," Joe said with a sense of great accomplishment. "Marisa is picking up a couple of shifts to see what she thinks of the place," he continued, arms crossed and visibly pleased with himself. Carson finally coaxed his legs to move to his favorite stool at the end of the bar. Settling in, he couldn't take his eyes off Marisa as she fluently worked the bar while attending to each guest as if they were the only person there. Joe sat next to Carson at the bar, resting his elbows on the copper bar top.

"A bit weird being on this side," he commented, as he too watched Marisa move with the precision of a ballerina.

"You're not quitting are you?" Carson asked with a hint of concern.

"No. Just looking to create a bit more balance in my schedule," Joe replied. Carson could feel his body began to relax while acknowledging that the world, as he has known it, had a story that was evolving as quickly as his.

Reaching over the bar, Joe grabbed a couple of cold mineral waters to share. "Look at it this way. We get to talk from the same side of the bar now," Joe said as he removed the caps from each bottle with the opener he carried in his back pocket. "So, where did we leave off last time we were together?" he asked as he tossed back the cold drink. "Wasn't forgiveness the next choice on your list?"

Carson paused before he answered, again wetting his dry mouth with the drink. "You're right. Forgiveness was the next of the choices. For starters, I've learned that others are much better at it than me," he said.

"What makes you believe that to be true?" Joe asked.

"Experience," Carson responded with a pained look on his face. Joe laughed out loud. "There is some truth in that statement. Answer this for me. How did it make you feel when someone gave you a second chance?" he asked.

Carson answered without hesitation, "Grateful—which is a new feeling for me, old friend." Together, they chuckled out loud.

"Consider this," Joe began. "When you hold second chances back from others, you create a type of prison—one for yourself and one for the other person. To give a second chance doesn't mean you have to forget. You just learn to let go of the offense against you, which opens the prison door for both parties." Carson nodded in agreement. "Sometimes, the person most in need of a second chance is you," Joe finished.

Joe reached into his pocket and removed a coin about the size of a half-dollar. Gently placing it on the bar top, Carson recognized the uniqueness of the coin. On the side facing him was a triangle with two X's in the center. Along the edges, surrounding the triangle, were the words *Unity, Recovery*, and *Service*. Carson was looking at an Alcoholics Anonymous coin which represented 20 years of sobriety. The confusion on Carson's face was apparent, prompting Joe to speak. "Don't look so confused. Haven't you ever seen an alcoholic run a bar?" he teased in a lighthearted manner. Carson's facial expressions spoke louder than any words forming in his mind. "Take a deep breath," Joe said. "It will be okay. I'm sharing this with you to show you I know a thing or two about second chances in life. It's a long story, dating back over 20 years, but the short version is this: My choices were killing me and destroying those I cared for the most. That is when I came across an ancient proverb that has had a tremendous impact on my life," he explained. Carson finally spoke.

"So, what was the proverb?" he asked, still eying the coin in measured disbelief.

Joe smiled and said, "Two are better than one, because there is a good return for their investment. Should one fall, the other is there to pick them up, but pity the one who falls and has no one to pick them up," he paused. "This really made sense to me after serving in the military."

Carson carefully digested the full range of their discussion and everything he had seen. His mind was racing with new and exciting thoughts for the first time in years. So much of what Clara and Sara had said to him began to make sense. The emptiness he had felt for so many years was beginning to come into focus and change shape. "Thank you for sharing. That took real courage," Carson said with a swell of deep appreciation.

"So help me interpret the last choice," Carson pleaded. "I would love your insights on what it means to serve others with honor," he said as he glanced at the drawer containing the medals he discovered. "I have come to understand that you know a thing or two about serving with honor."

Joe gave a Carson an uncomfortable stare while asking, "And how would you come to understand that?"

"You forget I'm an investigative journalist," Carson said with a smile, taking a long drink of his water. Joe's smile appeared from behind the beard.

"More like an investigative snoop," he said.

"It's not really snooping when you asked me to get the keys from the drawer. But now that it's out in the open, what's the story?" Carson asked calmly. Joe sat still for a moment as he twirled the now-empty bottle between his fingers.

"The story about the medals will have to be told another day. What you do need to know is serving others with honor is a high calling and an important choice we make in life. To serve in this manner is the act of putting others before you. You serve to show others the compassion, dignity, and respect they deserve," Joe began. "There is a difference between serving others with contempt verses serving others with honor," he continued. The look on Carson's face prompted Joe to finish. "We serve others with contempt when we feel an obligation to do something out of duty."

"But don't we have to suck it up at times and just do our jobs?" Carson asked.

"At times. The problem is that *sucking it up* is not a sustainable behavior. You can only fake it for so long until someone gets hurt," Joe replied

"That makes sense now," Carson said. "Remember back to the night that I wrote the article? I was struggling with the choice I needed to make. You told me if others get hurt, there is no honor in my actions. Until that moment, honor had never been part of my vocabulary," he admitted.

"And what does that mean to you now?" Joe asked.

"The day Clara picked me up from the hospital and took me to the park was the first time I saw Sara since the incident. Sara told me the story of the conversation she had with Clara the morning they were shot," Carson paused to catch his breath, given that was the first time he had said those words out loud. Just hearing the words spoken took his breath away for a brief moment, and he had to shake off feelings of guilt and shame. Regaining his composure, he continued, "Sara shared that Clara reiterated their purpose of serving others with integrity and honor. This act of selflessness, she explained, is serving for the right reason and showing others the dignity they deserve." Joe smiled as Carson related the story to him.

"This must feel like new territory for you. I can assure you, when you serve others in a way that honors them, you will find true meaning and significance," Joe affirmed.

"That seems like it can be more overwhelming than writing an advice column. I'm getting a bit anxious just talking about it," Carson said. "Next thing you know, I'll be writing poetry," he joked to mask his insecurity.

"Two things to remember here," Joe said, not letting him off the hook. "First, the old proverb I shared with you earlier—two are better than one. This essentially means that you should never try to embark on your journey by yourself." Joe watched Carson shake his head in agreement.

"And the second thing?" Carson asked, his full interest piqued by his renewed understanding.

"The second component I actually learned in AA. I am not in control, which means I am not first, but second—and at times even third," Joe explained. Carson's look showed he had more questions. "You are more than welcome to join me one night and explore these principles for yourself," Joe added.

"I can't believe I'm admitting this out loud, but I think I might enjoy that," Carson said, prompting an ear-to-ear grin to appear on Joe's face. Somehow, that beard was no longer Joe's most prominent feature, as far as Carson Stewart was concerned.

The
NEW BEGINNING

The two-inch headline above the fold told most of the story: *CONGRESSMAN RYAN BURR INDICTED.* The media frenzy was in full swing, running nonstop coverage of the Ryan Burr disgrace. Had he accepted the plan offered him to turn himself in and confess, he might have been shown some semblance of mercy in the public eye. His vigilant denial of any wrongdoing provided the first drop of blood in the sea of media sharks. It wasn't until the Malcolm Claire connection was exposed that Ryan Burr's world began to unravel in a colossal and irreparable way. Ryan Burr ultimately found he had nowhere to hide, and turned himself in.

Carson Stewart folded the paper under his arm as he rose from the park bench. Pulling his phone from his pocket, he located his contacts folder that now had several people listed—a new phenomenon for Carson. Locating Sara's picture, he tapped on her name, his heart missing a few beats. Within seconds, the enchanting voice of Sara Davis answered. "Hi there," she began with a lilt in her voice. "Guess you saw the paper?"

"Just finished reading it. Well done, I must add," he said.
"The phones have been ringing off the hook since the story broke," Sara reported. "This office has been in constant motion since I arrived."

"You must be slammed. I can let you go," Carson said as unconvincingly as possible.

"Nonsense. You are the break I needed," Sara said with a reassuring tone. "You going to be in D.C. anytime soon?" she asked subtly. "I could sure use another coffee with one Splenda."

"Nothing in D.C. for the foreseeable future, but I am going to be in Dallas soon. Possible job offer," he replied. Sara couldn't hide her excitement at hearing the news. The squeal she let out lifted the head of every staffer in her proximity.

"That is so exciting," she said, finally bringing the decibel level of her voice back to normal.

"It would be strange not living in the City after all these years, but it's time for a new beginning," he said.

"That is so wonderful, Carson," she offered, with more sincerity than he had ever heard coming from a woman.

"I should be thanking you and Clara. The two of you saw something in me that I couldn't. You saved my life, Sara," Carson whispered into the phone as he started walking through the park.

Sara was quiet on the other end as she took the time to let Carson's words wash over her. Her heart began to swell thinking about the new journey Carson was taking. The hope that his journey would include her brought tears to her eyes. "I would like to speak with your boss to let her know how much I appreciate her," Carson requested.

"Well, lucky for you I know people," Sara said in a playful voice.

"Does she have any travel to the City coming up?" Carson asked.

"No, but we are in Dallas in two weeks to begin our re-election prep work," Sara offered. "Maybe this will coincide with your travel." Carson smiled, realizing Sara still had not been told the news.

"Great," he said. "We can connect then. You should know, my new job offer is with Clara Becker. She is planning a book about her journey as a lawmaker, and asked if I would consider helping her write it." Sara's face beamed as she walked into Clara's office while still on the phone. Clara sat behind her desk, finishing up an email.

"I'm on the phone with Carson," Sara began, holding the phone away from her ear.

"Please do tell him I said howdy," Clara smiled, never looking up from her laptop.

"And when were you going to tell me about the book?" Sara asked, still holding the phone so Carson couldn't hear the conversation.

"Thought you would like to hear it directly from Carson," Clara said, looking up with a motherly smile. Sara again stood breathless, in complete awe of Clara's unending compassion.

The
EPILOGUE

The door to *Joe's Place* swung wide, ushering in the morning light. "Not quite open yet partner, but have a seat and I'll get to you in a sec," Joe said, his back to the door while he continued putting away clean glasses.

"Hello, Joseph."

Joe's arm froze mid-motion, while his whole body tensed in disbelief. There was no mistaking the voice he had not heard in twenty years. Glancing into the mirror behind the bar, he was able to catch a glimpse of the figure standing just inside the doorway. His heart began to race as he slowly replaced the glass he was holding, and turned to greet his visitor.

"Hello, Clara."

Walking up to the bar, Clara pulled out a stool and took a seat. Gently, she set down a tattered old book, a signed first edition of Hemingway's *For Whom the Bell Tolls*. The old inscription inside the front cover read, *To my Clara, You make the earth move. Joseph.* Just under the fading ink a new inscription read, *To my guardian angel, I am eternally grateful. Clara*

"I have an old book, looking for a new library," she said, acting as though she stopped by every day. "I've also heard you have the coldest mineral water in the city." Joe stood motionless, visually absorbing all that sat before him. The last time he saw Clara was the day he left for Ranger School. That was the day he had to make a choice between the alcohol that was consuming him or the love of his life. At the time, he thought hiding behind Ranger School would help ease the pain he was feeling inside. He was wrong. While the Rangers saved Joe from physical destruction, the shame he felt for letting Clara down consumed him for years. He justified his actions, increasing the intensity of his work and the great service he was offering to his country. Every mission deemed too dangerous by the State Department became Joe's calling card. For years, his family had no idea if he was still alive. Clara, however, never completely lost track of Joe through her government connections. Once Joe left the military, Clara heard he had successfully completed Alcoholics Anonymous and settled in New York—a tip from her dear friend Kyle Ellis, who always had a handle on the establishments in the City.

"Well, what brings you to a dive like this?" Joe asked in a shaky voice. Clara, sitting up straight on her barstool, looked around the bar.

"This looks more like a dump than a dive," she said, cracking a subtle smile. "Actually, I felt it important to say thank you face-to-face," she offered. Joe's head dipped to break eye contact for a moment and disguise the tears blurring his vision of Clara.

"Thank me for what? Not sure I know what you are talking about," he said, his voice still not at full strength.

"Nonsense," she replied with the full force of her official voice. "You do remember I am a United States congresswoman and you were a United States ranger. I have my resources and you have yours," she said with a smile. "I know it was you who saved my life, along with the life of your niece."

Joe began to move towards Clara, leaning behind the bar to remove a cold mineral water. He straightened up, popped the cap and poured the contents into a frosted mug. "It took the FBI a fair amount of time before they were able to piece together what truly happened that day on the Capitol steps," Clara began, gratefully accepting the drink. "It seems the madman shooter who jumped the barricade only fired three shots, despite the evidence that five shots were fired. The fourth bullet took out the madman in a single shot, and according to the FBI, that shot was fired from roughly 1800 yards away."

Taking a sip of the mineral water in front of her, Clara smiled. "That *is* pretty good water." She sat up straight and continued, "It was the second assassin who was the biggest mystery, and the FBI was not able to piece it together without the help of the CIA. Turns out that the CIA lost track of a terrorist assassin from South America and had put their best agents on the search. They were reaching dead ends, until they received an anonymous tip detailing where to find the body. Once they located the body of the assassin, they found enough evidence to connect him to the situation at the Capitol. Seems he had it in for me in a big way—or perhaps it was the $5 million he was being paid to kill me," she continued. "Didn't take long to trace the money through six different offshore accounts before we tagged Malcolm Claire for financing the hit." Joe stood quietly as Clara recounted the final detail of the case. "Both agencies have finished the investigation, with no definitive leads to the shooter who saved my life and took out the assassins with those last two bullets." Even his beard could not conceal the deep shade of red creeping up Joe's face. "There's only one sharpshooter I know, who could have pulled that off," Clara said, finishing her water.

"I always knew I had a guardian angel, just didn't think it would be you when I needed it most. Thank you, Joseph," she said simply, her eyes filled with deep sincerity. "And don't worry. The FBI has stopped looking for the other shooter, suspecting it to be a covert operation of the CIA."

"How is Sara?" Joe quickly changed the subject, embarrassed that his protective kindness was exposed.

"She is fully recovered and stronger than ever," Clara beamed. "You should consider telling her who you are," she offered gently.

"You know she was here, in the bar, with Carson the night they met for dinner. I recognized her right away and my heart stopped in my chest. Just like it did when you walked into my bar today," Joe added. "Besides, she thinks I was killed in the Middle East. It was just easier to remain silent."

"Things with Carson are moving forward. She is going to need someone to walk her down the aisle one day soon. That needs to be you, Joseph," Clara stated in a very matter-of-fact tone. "And maybe Carson can finally make use of that ring," she said softly, eying his finger.

Joe began to polish the bar top out of nervous habit. "I wouldn't know what to say," he mumbled.

"Good grief," Clara yelled. "Just tell her who you are. She is your family. I am heading to Dallas in two days. Sara is already there along with Carson. Here is a ticket. Surely you can find someone to cover the bar for a week or so," she said with a wry smile.

Joe looked at the ticket, and then at Clara. Clara put the ticket inside the old book and slid them both across the bar until they touched his fingertips. Slowly he closed his hand over the old leather cover he hadn't felt in years. Looking up, he simply said, "Thank you, Clara. I just might."

Being a native of Dallas had its perks, especially when it came to finding the hidden culinary treasures of the city's dining scene. During law school at SMU, Sara got to know all the best places to enjoy a meal within walking distance of the school. When Carson, Clara, and Sara walked into *Bubba's*, a 1950s converted gas station, the aroma of fried chicken filled the air. Most days of the week, the line at the counter was 20-30 deep with locals anticipating some of the best comfort food in the state of Texas. Today happened to be unusually quiet, as the three of them, along with Clara's security detail, were the only people in the art deco restaurant.

The conversation was focused on Clara's book, which only had a working title at the moment. *The Lawmaker* was Carson's idea, and Clara liked the way it sounded. As the group continued to sketch the outline for the book, no one noticed the tall, muscular man entering the dining room. Carson and Clara were the first to spot him, as they were facing the entrance. Sara, whose back was to the door, did not realize someone had entered the room. Carson stopped what he was doing and stared in disbelief. He did a double take before recognition dawned upon his face. Sliding out of his seat, he went to greet his old friend in the middle of the room. Sara, taking notice that something was going on, turned to see Carson embrace Joe with an enormous bear hug. Finishing his embrace, Carson turned to Sara and was about to speak, when he was interrupted. "Hello, Sara. I'm your uncle, Joseph. There is a story I need to share with you. With your trust, I would like to discover how the story ends." Joe let the words hang in the air as he stood breathlessly, completely out of his element. Without hesitation, Sara ran to fully embrace Joe, burying her head deep into his chest.

Looking up, she smiled, "A wise man once said that the best way to trust someone is to trust him." Stepping back, she added, "Actually, make that two very wise men." The steady stream of tears was infectious, sweeping everyone in the small dining room into the emotional reunion. Looking Joe directly in his tear-soaked eyes, Sara smiled and whispered, "This story isn't ending; it is just beginning. I love you, Uncle Joe. Welcome home."

Learning Points:
THE NEWSMAKER

1. Lead with Love
Focus the lead story in life on loving others. Our life has a narrative or storyline. In this storyline we have two choices: a life of judgment, or a life of love.

2. Forgive Frequently
The power of the second chance. Forgiveness is not about forgetting, but about letting go. When we extend second chances, we enhance our ability to influence others, which only increases our leadership potential.

3. Serve with Honor
Live life in a deliberate way. To serve with honor is to show others the respect and dignity they deserve. When we serve with honor we leave the one we serve in a better place, being lifted to a place of honor.

4. Finding True Joy

A life focused only on self is a life filled with empty joy. A meaningful purpose in life will always be externally focused towards others. When we focus our life energy, our talents, and even our resources in the direction of serving others with honor; there we find true joy.

5. Seeking Truth

Truth is anchored to a fixed set of morals and principles. Truth does not deceive.

6. Finding Your Purpose

Your purpose is why you are here. Everyone has a purpose. Think of purpose as a journey to someplace deliberate. Ask these questions, *"What are my gifts and talents, and what do I really value most?"*

7. The Newsmaker:

A person who impacts the larger public conversation in an effort to model positive change in the community.

ACKNOWLEDGMENTS

Each day I become increasingly more appreciative for key people in my life. It would be difficult to imagine doing life without them. Yet, it takes an email from my editor to remind me to write the acknowledgment page to finish up the book. I am embarrassed to say I could do a better job at acknowledging how much I appreciate those people in my life. Heck, each day I write a new chapter in the story of my life; shouldn't I be writing an acknowledgment page for those moments also? After all, it is important to let people know how much you appreciate them.

The process of writing a book is interesting. The sheer amount of moving parts and pieces to take a book from concept to bookshelf is staggering. *The Newsmaker* is my third book, and I am still amazed at the amount of work required to bring a book to market. In each moving part of the process is a key individual or team of individuals working to ensure the author's success. It is a humbling experience.

What I lack as a writer I hope to make up as a storyteller. That is where a great editor comes in. Within a few weeks of the first words of *The Newsmaker* being typed on my computer, I was informed of a new editorial manager, Jana Good, and a new team editor, Mindi Bach. My first reaction was terror, then anxiety for both. After the first couple of chapters it became apparent Mindi was a true partner in making sure the story in my head made it to print. Both ladies bring out the best in others with their world-class work. I appreciate their heart.

As with any writing project, there is always a support team providing encouragement and feedback along the way. People like Leslie Miller provided the coaching and counsel for life, which in turn helped craft some of the tougher scenes in the story. I appreciate her dedication.

Daniel Morris is my ever-present sounding board for the key learning points throughout the story. His unwavering support and counsel has provided countless inspiration for the characters on the pages of this book. I appreciate his in-sight.

My daughter, Allison, has been one of my biggest fans as well as my travel buddy. While doing research for the book she accompanied me to New York City and endured the geeky process of book research with her dad. She inspires me to be a better dad. I appreciate her encouragement.

My youngest son, Brendan, has always been an encourager when it comes to my writing. Together, we have shared our fair share of second chances. His smile and willingness to face every day, one day at a time, is inspiring to watch. I appreciate his courage.

My beautiful bride, Dee, is my rock here on Earth. Her determination and drive to be the best she can be at everything she tackles is motivation. Her willingness to do life with me for all these years is proof miracles are still happening. Her patience with me as I continue my journey to love and honor her as we do life together is at the core of why I love her as much as I do. I appreciate everything about her.

Tony Bridwell

As an author, international speaker, consultant and coach, Tony Bridwell has been making a difference at some of the world's largest organizations for the past 20 years. He is the author of *The Maker* series, former Chief People Officer of Brinker International and a current partner with a global consulting firm.

Tony is a highly recognized thought leader in corporate culture, L&D, and human resources, being named 2015 HR Executive of the Year by DallasHR (the local SHRM affiliate) and also receiving the 2015 Strategic Leadership Award from Strategic Excellence HR.

Tony has been a facilitator and featured speaker for audiences of several thousand people and has presented for multiple conferences and associations, including the CHRO Exchange, DallasHR (SHRM), the HRSouthwest Conference, ATD San Diego, and the California Restaurant Association. Tony is also a member of SHRM and serves on the board of directors for Unlimited Partnerships and Taylor's Gift Foundation.

When he is not spending time with his family, Tony turns his efforts toward mentoring a small group of young men, cycling, and writing. With three grown children and two dogs, Tony and his wife, Dee, have called the Dallas area home for almost 30 years.

More from Tony Bridwell,

The Kingmaker

63984784R00102

Made in the USA
Middletown, DE
12 February 2018